Reuters Handbook for Journalists

Reuters Handbook for Journalists

Ian Macdowall

BUTTERWORTH
HEINEMANN

Butterworth-Heinemann Ltd
Linacre House, Jordan Hill, Oxford OX2 8DP

 PART OF REED INTERNATIONAL BOOKS

OXFORD   LONDON   BOSTON
MUNICH   NEW DELHI   SINGAPORE   SYDNEY
TOKYO   TORONTO   WELLINGTON

First published 1992

© Reuters Ltd 1992

Editorial Adviser: F. W. Hodgson

British Library Cataloguing in Publication Data
Macdowall, Ian
    Reuters Handbook for Journalists
    I. Title
    070.4
ISBN 0 7506 0551 0

Library of Congress Cataloguing in Publication Data
Macdowall, Ian.
    Reuters handbook for journalists/Ian Macdowall.
    p.   cm.
    ISBN 0 7506 0551 0
    1. Reuters Ltd.   2. Journalism – Handbooks, manuals, etc.
    3. Reporters and reporting – Great Britain.   I. Reuters Ltd.
    II. Title.
    PN5111.R4M34   1992
    070.4–dc20   92–5673

Printed and bound in Great Britain by
Redwood Press, Melksham, Wiltshire

Dedication

The reputation of Reuters rests on its accuracy, speed and reliability.

This handbook was compiled by the late Ian Macdowall, Chief News Editor of Reuters, for the reporters and editors of our international news gathering network. It was intended not only as a work of reference, but also as an aid to increasing the clarity, precision and consistency of our reporting across the whole spectrum of our news operations. Shortly before his death in December 1991, Macdowall revised the contents for a wider public.

Macdowall joined Reuters in 1957 from the *Glasgow Herald*. He had an Oxford degree in English and – more to the point, he used to say – a four-year apprenticeship in the most demanding school of Scottish newspaper journalism. He worked with Reuters for 33 years as sub-editor, foreign correspondent and Chief News Editor. As a reporter, he covered three decades of trouble-spots including the Soviet intervention in Czechoslovakia, Black September in Jordan and the dismantling of the Berlin Wall. As an editor, he established Reuters Editorial Quality Unit, which monitors the work of all the agency's news services.

This book is a memorial to Ian Macdowall's passionate, life-long commitment to the highest standards of news writing.

It is also dedicated, as Macdowall himself wanted, to those journalists who, in the last 25 years, have been killed in combat zones in the service of Reuters and Visnews, the international television news agency:

Bruce Piggot, Vietnam	1968
Ron Laramy, Vietnam	1968
Najmul Hasan, Iran	1983
Willie Vicoy, Philippines	1986
Roberto Navas Alvarez, El Salvador	1989
George Semerjian, Lebanon	1990

Mark Wood
Editor-in-Chief

Preface

News agencies have traditionally been wholesalers of news, supplying information to the press and the electronic media – clients with diverse needs, editorial objectives and political opinions.

In the past 20 years or so, Reuters and other information providers have developed retail services, selling economic news in particular direct to the end user in the booming business markets. But the principles which govern both traditional services to the media and newer services to the financial community remain the same. It is the aim of this book to explain both these principles and how they should be applied in practice.

This manual is descriptive not prescriptive. Reuters does not seek to lay down standards which other news agencies should follow. This book simply expounds the rules which Reuter journalists should follow in reporting the news. It is for the reader of this book to decide to what extent these rules are applicable to his or her work. But it is worth noting that, allowing for differences of terminology, the rules set down here are much the same for other major international news agencies such as Agence France-Presse and Associated Press, as well as Reuters.

The cardinal principle which should underlie the work of any news agency is honesty. Its file should be accurate as to fact and balanced as to the selection of facts and of background and interpretation used in putting these facts in context. A corollary of this is a readiness to correct any significant error fully, frankly and quickly.

Precise sourcing is essential to any news agency story. The reader should never have to ask: 'How does Reuters (or AFP or AP) know this to be true?'

Total impartiality is an ideal which is in practice very difficult if not impossible to attain. Any news agency journalist is conditioned by his or her nationality, education, culture, religion or personal beliefs. The honest journalist will be conscious of these factors and will not allow them to influence the presentation of a story.

The main virtue of an agency story, after accuracy and balance, is speed. News agency copy has a very short shelf life. The other essential quality of the agency file is clarity. Copy should be written in simple, direct language which can be assimilated quickly, which goes straight to the heart of the story and in which, as a general rule, facts are marshalled in logical sequence according to their relative importance.

This book differs from the traditional news agency or newspaper style book in that it includes not only rules for spelling and grammar but also guidance on how a news agency file should be structured and thumbnail explanations of some international political issues which are regularly in the news.

The book is based in part upon my own experience of 33 years – 11 of them as Chief News Editor – as a Reuter correspondent, sub-editor and editorial executive. But it owes more to the traditions laid down by generations of Reuter journalists and to contributions made by individual correspondents and sub-editors to the *Reuter Handbook*. to the *Reuter Handbook*.

Particular thanks are due to Andrew Waller, who compiled the technical glossary.

Ian Macdowall

Introduction

For a journalist there is more to the right word than rounding off a fine description or filling out a headline, important though these functions are. The right word has to convey to the reader unambiguously and without confusion what the writer is trying to say.

Some words – and uses of words – are so pivotal in written communication that if they are wrongly or sloppily used or misunderstood the whole point of a report or an article can be lost. It might be a word on which hinges a vital definition; or a choice between confusingly similar words of different meaning. The problem might be the best way to explain clearly a piece of technical jargon, to iron out a surfeit of abbreviations, or simply to get right the style and title of some important person. A slip-up in any of these areas of word use can baffle or annoy readers.

Every day journalists grapple with this problem of textual accuracy and consistency both in the objective world of reporting and in the subjective world of comment and analysis.

The pitfalls are endless. Not only are some words popularly misused, or have acquired new or alternative uses; reporters and writers themselves have personal blind spots about spellings and meanings. Similar words can get their meanings transposed; alternative spellings of some words exist, but occasionally with shifts of meaning; certain technical words have been adopted into general use or have acquired a vogue, but have disputed meanings.

Abbreviations and acronyms are a world on their own: how to render them consistently, where to use capitals, where lower case and full points . . . and when to use them. Consistency is likewise needed in foreign words and place names; some names are rendered so differently that it may seem they are two entirely different places.

Financial terms at a time when countries' economies are under the microscope are a particular source of misuse and bafflement; traps await the unwary in the use of trade names; there is the problem of which Americanisms are acceptable to the reader.

Some newspapers and news agencies produce a style sheet of usage to save themselves from the bigger traps and inconsistencies. Reuters, the international news organisation, has developed a keen sense of the problems of style and word accuracy in the course of collecting news and distributing it to subscriber newspapers round the world. As a result its house style guide has grown in response to the varied demands of its services until it has become a leading work of reference in its own right, with perhaps the greatest penetration and widest coverage of all news writing style books.

I feel that today, despite the oddities and age-old sanctity of some house styles, there is enough common – and commonsense – ground, and enough demand, to make news writing style worth tackling in a general handbook for the use of journalists and newspapers across the board in the English-speaking world. What better basis for this than the Reuters Style Guide? So Reuters own compilation on news style goes public as *Reuters Handbook for Journalists*. I commend it to all journalists.

F. W. Hodgson
Editor, Butterworth-Heinemann Media List

A

a, an Use *a* before a word which begins with the sound of a consonant, e.g. *a gun, a historian, a hotel, a hysterectomy, a NATO member, a one-armed man, a U.N. member.* Use *an* before a word which begins with the sound of a vowel, e.g. *an heir, an honour, an OPEC member.*

abbreviations You should use abbreviations for the sake of brevity but never at the expense of clarity. A reader should not have to check back to find out what an abbreviation means.

It is better to use a generic term, e.g *the company* or *the organisation*, than to stud a story with abbreviations, especially where more than one or two sets of initials are involved.

Abbreviations in common use are given under their alphabetical entries.

While some common abbreviations, e.g. *AIDS, NATO,* should be used alone at first reference, with the full name given later in the story, it is usually better to give the full name at first reference and to use the abbreviation for later references.

House styles vary on whether or not to use full stops after each initial in an abbreviation. Generally they are used when an abbreviation consists of only two initials, e.g. *U.S.*, *U.N.*, but not when it consists of three or more initials, e.g. *IBM*, *UNICEF*, or is an acronym (**q.v.**) composed of initial syllables, e.g. *Aramco, Gestapo.*

If initials are well known, e.g. *PLO, SALT,* do not bracket the initials after the first full reference. You may write *The Palestine Liberation Organisation has sent two envoys . . .* and then *A PLO statement said the two men would. . . .*

But if the institution is little known, and especially if the second reference does not follow soon after the first, bracket the initials after the first reference, e.g. *The Western European Union (WEU) decided on Tuesday. . . .*

In the case of foreign groups, where the word order changes in English translation, you should bracket the initials, e.g. *the Sandinista National Liberation Front (FSLN).*

Do not bracket initials after a first full reference if you are not going to use the initials again lower in the story.

Form the plural of abbreviations by adding a lower-case *s* without any apostrophe, e.g. *ICBMs* not *ICBM's* or *ICBMS.*

Use capital letters when abbreviating capitalised words, lower case for uncapitalised phrases, e.g. *ASEAN* but *mph, bpd.*

-able   Words ending in a silent *e* normally drop it before *-able*, e.g. *arguable.* But words ending in *-ce* or *-ge* do not, e.g. *changeable.*

ABM   anti-ballistic missile.

abortion   Choose your words with care on this highly emotive subject. Unless quoting someone, refer to aborted foetuses rather than unborn babies. Describe those campaigning for a woman's right to have an abortion as pro-choice rather than pro-abortion, since they are not advocating more abortions per se but the right to have choice.

academic titles   Capitalise when they accompany a personal name; otherwise use lower case, e.g. *Professor John Smith* but *the history professor.*

accommodate, accommodation   Two ms, not *accomodate, accomodation.*

account dealing   The British practice of buying and selling a parcel of shares within the same stock exchange account period, i.e. before deals are settled. Investors dealing in this way settle only the difference between buying and selling prices, plus commission on purchases.

accusations If an accusation has been denied, ensure that any subsequent or follow-up stories that repeat the accusation also repeat the denial.

Achilles' heel, tendon Note apostrophe.

acknowledgment Not *acknowledgement.*

acre To convert roughly to hectares multiply by 2 and divide by 5; to convert precisely multiply by 0.405.

acronym A word formed from the initial letters or syllables of other words, e.g. *radar – radio detection and ranging.* An acronym formed from initial letters is usually capitalised throughout, e.g. *AIDS, NATO,* while one formed from initial syllables normally has only the first letter in upper case, e.g. Saudi *Aramco – Arabian American Oil Company.*

acting Not capitalised in titles, e.g. *acting Governor John Smith.*

AD Anno Domini (in the year of our Lord). Strictly speaking, it should precede the date, e.g. *AD 73,* although in practice most publications use the form 73 AD. House styles vary on whether to put a space between the year and the AD.

additional *more* is shorter and usually better.

adjectives These tend to be the crutch of a lazy journalist seeking to inject drama into a story. Use them sparingly. Avoid adjectives that imply a judgment, e.g. *a hard-line speech, a glowing tribute, a staunch conservative.* Depending on where they stand, some people might consider the speech moderate, the tribute fulsome or the conservative a die-hard reactionary.

For hyphenation of adjectives, see **punctuation.**

administration Use lower case, e.g. *the Bush administration.*

admit Use with care. If you say someone admitted something you imply that it had previously been concealed or that there is an element of guilt. *Said* is usually better.

admiral Hyphenate *rear-admiral* and *vice-admiral.* At second reference just *admiral.* A vice-admiral outranks a rear-admiral.

ADR   American Depositary Receipt (not Depository). This is a certificate issued by U.S. banks to facilitate trading in foreign stocks and shares. It entitles the holder to all dividends and capital gains.

advancer   A story filed two or three days before a scheduled event (or even earlier in the case of a feature). It should take a broad-brush approach, assessing the issues and personalities involved, with appropriate analysis and background. A curtainraiser (**q.v.**), which is filed just before an event, should give more detail about the timetable of meetings, venue, security arrangements, etc.

adverbs   Like adjectives (**q.v.**), they should be used sparingly. Avoid adverbs that imply a judgment, e.g. *generously, harshly, sternly*.
  Put the adverb between the auxiliary verb and the past participle, **e.g.** *France has already refused . . .* not *France already has refused . . .*
  Resist the growing tendency to add unnecessary adverbs to verbs, e.g. *check (out), consult (with), fill (up), meet (up with), rest (up), sound (out), start (up), tighten (up), try (out).*
  For the use of hyphens in adverbs, see **punctuation**.

adviser   Not *advisor*. But *advisory*.

aerodrome   Use *airfield*.

aeroplane   Use *aircraft*.

affect, effect   *Affect* is a verb meaning *to influence*; *effect* is usually a noun meaning *outcome* or *consequence*, e.g. *The effect of the decision will be to affect the company's decision. Effect* as verb means to accomplish, e.g. *He effected his escape with the aid of his wife. Affect* is a vague word; seek a more precise one. *Effect* is usually word-spinning. *He escaped . . .* is simpler.

Afghanistan   When Soviet troops intervened in Afghanistan in 1979 to install Babrak Karmal as head of the Communist government in Kabul, the United States, Saudi Arabia and other Arab states sent arms through Pakistan to support Islamic mujahideen rebels. The seven main guerrilla groups are based in the north Pakistani city of Peshawar. Small Shia groups operate from Iran. More than three million Afghan refugees live in camps in Pakistan and two million in Iran. Soviet troops withdrew in 1989 under the 1988 Geneva Accords. Moscow and Washington agreed in 1991 to halt arms shipments to the two sides by January 1, 1992, and backed a United Nations plan for talks on an interim government to take power in Kabul and hold elections. President Najibullah (one word), who took over from Karmal in 1986, sought a continuing role for the ruling party, renamed the Watan (Homeland) Party in 1990. The exile Afghan interim government, set up in Peshawar in 1989, was split between groups wanting a negotiated settlement and those pledged to fight on. Former King Zahir Shah, deposed in a coup in 1973, lives in Rome.

AFL-CIO   American Federation of Labour-Congress of Industrial Organisations.

Africa   Be careful in using the term *Black Africa* unless you are quoting someone. South Africa is a white-ruled state but has a large black majority. Some so-called Black African states are Arab-ruled. A geographical term like *sub-Saharan Africa* is often better.

Afrikaner   A white South African, usually of Dutch descent.

Afrikaans   The language spoken by Afrikaners.

age   *The 66-year-old president* or *an 18-year-old youth* are fine. But avoid the usage *the 66-year-old Jones* which suggests he is being distinguished from another, 65-year-old Jones. *Jones, who is 66*, or just *Jones, 66*, is simpler.

ageing   Not *aging*.

agree   You *agree on (or to) a proposal* not *agree a proposal*.

AIDS   Acronym for acquired immune deficiency syndrome, in which a virus attacks the body's immune system, gradually eliminating the victim's ability to fight infection and disease. The initials should be used by themselves at first reference with the full name given lower in the story. Use *AIDS* rather than *HIV*, which is the scientific name for the virus that causes the disease, the human immunodeficiency virus. Use the phrase *infected with AIDS* or *infected with the AIDS virus* rather than *AIDS-positive* or *HIV-positive*, which are medical terms for someone infected with the AIDS virus. Stories must often differentiate between people infected but without visible symptoms and people with the advanced disease. But in fact a person has AIDS as soon as he or she becomes infected, whether or not symptoms are visible. However, to differentiate, you may use terms such as *an AIDS carrier, infected, without symptoms* or *at an early stage of infection* as opposed to *an AIDS patient, advanced disease, advanced*

AIDS symptoms, with full-blown AIDS and so forth. AIDS is not spread through casual contact but always by intimate sexual contact, by the sharing of needles by drug addicts, by blood transfusions or from a mother to her infant at birth.

See **medical stories** on the need for caution in handling stories about reputed cures for AIDS.

Airbus   One word, capitalised, unhyphenated.

aircraft   Most airliners and military aircraft are jets so there is normally no need to specify that an aircraft is a jet.

Warplane is one word, by analogy with warship. Do not use the word *airplane* or the term *fighter jet*.

Capitalise but do not quote the names of aircraft, e.g. *Concorde, Flogger, Stealth, Tomcat*. When the number designating an aircraft is preceded by a letter or letters, hyphenate, e.g. *Boeing 747* but *DC-10, F-111*. Be specific when giving aircraft models in economic stories (e.g. *Boeing 747-400* not just *Boeing 747*) as there are cost differences.

For makers' names the accepted guide is the form given in Jane's *All the World's Aircraft*, e.g. *MiG-21*.

Give numerals for aircraft speeds, e.g. *Mach 1* not *Mach one*.

air crashes   When reporting an air crash the first priority is to establish the airline and aircraft involved, its flight number and route and the number of passengers and crew, with estimates of casualties. Check the availability of a passenger list. Remember that babies are sometimes not listed. Check on weather conditions in the crash area.

Graphic descriptions of a crash and its aftermath are welcome. But be wary of any eyewitness report or other statement not covered by privilege that appears to impute blame to any party. Use discretion in describing a crash scene. Bodies may be dismembered and entrails hanging from trees. Such things are best left to the imagination.

air force   House styles vary but most editors prefer two words.

airlines   Airlines vary widely in their use of *air line(s)* or *airline(s)* or *airways* as part of their name. This is a list of the ones most frequently used and of those that cause problems over spelling. It gives both the short name of the airline and, with the bracketed material, a full reference. It also gives the designator by which the airline is listed in timetables. For a full list see the ABC *World Airways Guide*.

Aer Lingus (Plc) – EI – Republic of Ireland
Aeroflot – SU – CIS
Aerolineas Argentinas – AR – Argentina
Aeromexico (Aerovias de Mexico) – AM – Mexico
Air Afrique – RK – an Abidjan-based company owned by a consortium of 10 African states
Air Algerie – AH – Algeria
Air Canada – AC
Air China – CA – China, international
Air France – AF – France
Air-India (note hyphen) – AI – India
Air Inter – AI – France, domestic
Air Lanka (Ltd) – UL – Sri Lanka
Air New Zealand – NZ
Alitalia – AZ – Italy
All Nippon Airways (Co Ltd) – NH – Japan
American Airlines (Inc) – AA (see also separate entry)
Ariana Afghan Airlines – FG
Austrian Airlines – OS
Avianca – AV – Colombia
Biman (Bangladesh Airlines) – BG
British Airways – BA
CAAC, the Chinese civil aviation authority which is the holding company for China's international carrier, Air China, and seven regional carriers:
    China Eastern Airlines – MU
    China General Aviation Corporation – GP
    China Northern Airlines – CG
    China Northwest Airlines – WH
    China Southern Airlines – CZ
    China Southwest Airlines – SZ
    Xinjiang Airlines – XO
Cathay Pacific (Airways Ltd) – CX – Hong Kong-based
China Airlines (Ltd of Taiwan) – CI
Continental Airlines (Inc) – CO – U.S.-based
Cruzeiro do Sul – SC – Brazil
CSA – OK – Czechoslovakia
Cubana – CU – Cuba
Danair (A/S) – DX – Denmark
Delta Airlines (Inc) – DL – U.S.-based
Dragonair – KA – Hong Kong

Eastern Air Lines (Inc) – EA – U.S.-based
Egyptair – MS – Egypt
El Al (Israeli Airlines Ltd) – LY
Ethiopian Airlines – ET
Finnair – AY – Finland
Garuda Indonesia – GA
Ghana Airways (Corp) – GH
Gulf Air (Company G.S.C.) – GF
Hang Khong Viet Nam – VN – Vietnam
Iberia – IB – Spain
Icelandair – FI – Iceland
Indian Airlines – IC – India, domestic
Iran Air – IR – Iran
Japan Airlines (Co Ltd) – JL
JAT – JU – Yugoslavia
Kenya Airways – KQ
KLM Royal Dutch Airlines – KL
Korean Air – KE – South Korea
Kuwait Airways (Corp) – KU
LAB (Lloyd Aereo Boliviano SA) – LB – Bolivia
LAN-Chile (SA) – LA – Chile
LOT Polish Airlines – LO
Lufthansa German Airlines (Deutsche Lufthansa AG) – LH
MAS (Malaysian Airline System Bhd) – MH
Malev Hungarian Airlines – MA
MEA (Middle East Airlines) – ME – Beirut-based
Nigeria Airways (Ltd) – WT
Northwest Airlines (Inc) – NW – U.S.-based
Olympic Airways – OA – Greece
PIA (Pakistan International Airlines) – PK
Philippine Airlines – PR
Qantas Airways (Ltd) – QF – Australia
Royal Air Maroc – AT – Morocco
Royal Jordanian Airline – RJ
Sabena World Airlines – SN – Belgium
SAS (Scandinavian Airlines System) – SK
Saudia – SV – Saudi Arabia
SIA (Singapore Airlines Ltd) – SQ
SAA (South African Airways) – SA
Sudan Airways – SD
Swissair – SR – Switzerland

Syrian Arab Airlines – RB
TAP (Air Portugal) – TP
Tarom – RO – Romania
Thai Airways International Ltd – TG
TWA (Trans World Airlines Inc) – TW U.S.-based
Turkish Airlines (Inc) – TK
Uganda Airlines (Corp) – QU
United Airlines (Inc) – UA – U.S.-based
USAir (Inc) – US – U.S.-based
UTA (Union de Transports Aeriens) – UT – France
Varig Brazilian Airlines – RG
VIASA – VA Venezuela
Virgin Air (Inc) – ZP – Virgin Islands
Virgin Atlantic Airways (Inc) – VS – Britain
Zambia Airways (Corp) – QZ

airlift Do not use as a synonym for *fly*, e.g. *The injured man was airlifted to hospital.* Reserve it for shuttle services, e.g. *The United States airlifted 50,000 troops to the Gulf.*

airplane Use *aircraft*.

air raid Two words.

alibi Not a synonym for an excuse. It means a claim to have been elsewhere at the time of an alleged offence.

all right Not *alright*.

All Saints' Day November 1. Note apostrophe.

Allahu Akbar – *God is Greater* (not, as often written, *God is Great*), a common Moslem rallying cry. Also chanted when Moslems perform their five daily prayers.

allege Use with great care. Do not report allegations without saying who made them. Use of the word *alleged* before a defamatory statement does not provide immunity against an action for libel.

alternate, alternative *Alternate* means that A and B take turns, *alternative* that you have a choice between A and B. When you see the word *alternative*, ask whether *other* would not be preferable.

altitudes Convert metres to feet not yards when giving altitudes. The height of mountains should be converted precisely.

aluminium Not *aluminum*, which is American usage.

Alzheimer's disease   A progressive, incurable and disabling disease leading to severe dementia. Although it usually occurs in elderly people it is not synonymous with dementia or senility.

a.m.   Time: ante meridiem (before noon) e.g. *6 a.m.*

AM   The amplitude modulation method of radio transmission.

ambassador   House styles vary but most prefer lower case, e.g. *the British ambassador, Peter Williams*, or *U.S. ambassador Shirley Temple Black.* An envoy is an ambassador *to* a country but *in* a capital, e.g. *The French ambassador to Israel, the Danish ambassador in Bangkok.*

ambience   A vogue word meaning *atmosphere*; a shade pretentious for use in a hard news story.

American   As a noun this may be used to describe a U.S. citizen. *North American* includes Canadians. *Latin American* covers everyone from the Rio Grande to Cape Horn apart from the Caribbean, but *South American* excludes Mexicans and citizens of the Central American states.

American airlines   Use *U.S.-based airlines* when referring to U.S. airline companies. Reserve use of the term *American Airlines* (both upper case) for the company of that name.

Americanisms   Use of words with peculiarly American meanings or of American grammatical structures can cause readers problems in countries where English English is taught. The following list gives some words and usages to be avoided:

AVOID	PREFER
airplane	aircraft
to appeal	to appeal against
to author	to write
downtown	central
facility	military base, factory
fall	autumn
gasoline	petrol
gridlock	deadlock (in metaphorical sense)
to gun down	to shoot
to hand someone a defeat	to beat
heist	robbery
to headquarter	to base
pay hike	pay rise

to hospitalize	to enter hospital
to host a dinner	to give a dinner
to impact	to affect
lawmakers	congressmen/senators
legislators	congressmen/senators
to meet with	to meet
moot	debatable
to move to do something	to do something
the nation's capital	Washington
ouster	dismissal, ousting
presently	currently
proponent	supporter
rhetoric	language
sanction	to approve or to penalise
shot to death	shot dead
to slate	to criticise
straight	successive
to stump	to campaign for
to table	either to put forward or to postpone discussion of
to task with	to ask to
to throw rocks	to throw stones
to visit with	to visit

Also, avoid giving people's middle initials.

America's Cup   A yachting trophy. Note apostrophe.

among, between   Use *between* in referring to a series of bilateral contacts, e.g. *relations between the NATO states*. Use *among* for a looser, collective linkage, e.g. *Among issues discussed were. . . .*

ampersand   Use the ampersand if it forms part of a company name, e.g. *P&O*.

anaesthesia   Not *anesthesia*.

analysts   As a source this is so vague as to be almost meaningless. Be as specific as possible, e.g. *diplomatic analysts, military analysts, money market analysts, motor industry analysts*. See **sourcing**.

and/but   When you see *but* linking clauses, stop and consider whether *and* would not be more suitable. Journalists often tend to use *but* when there is no conflict or contrast.

Anglican Church   Queen Elizabeth is head of the Church of England. The Archbishop of Canterbury is Primate of All England and head of the worldwide Anglican community, which has about 70 million members. The Archbishop of York is Primate of England. Do not use honorifics such as *Most Reverend* or *Right Reverend*. At first reference either *the Archbishop of Canterbury, (Dr) George Carey*, or simply *The Archbishop of Canterbury*, with the name in the next paragraph. At subsequent references *the archbishop* or *(Dr) Carey*. House style determines whether you use the Dr or not.

animals   Use the neutral pronoun *it* for animals unless their sex is clear, e.g. *The dog bit its owner, The stallion tossed his head, Judy the parrot escaped from her cage.*

announcements   Only competent authorities make *announcements*. Others simply *say* or *make statements*. Do not write *it was announced* unless in the next sentence or paragraph you say who made the announcement.

another   Do not write *Six men were killed and another 23 wounded*. It's *Six men were killed and 23 wounded*.

ANPA formats   The American Newspaper Publishers' Association gave its acronym to two sequences of prefatory information about stories, designed to help systems route and index them. The best known is *ANPA 1312*. Information such as story number, date and time, priority, category code and keyboard is placed in predetermined fields.

Antarctic   Not *Antarctic*.

anti-   When the second element of a word beginning with *anti-* starts with a capital, hyphenate, e.g. *anti-Semitism*.

anticipate, expect   These are not synonyms. If you *anticipate* something you not only expect it but also take precautionary action to deal with it.

apostrophes   See **punctuation**.

appeal   You *appeal against* a verdict, not *appeal* the verdict.

appraise, apprise   To *appraise* is to put a value on, to *apprise* is to inform.

approximately   Use *about*.

APR annual percentage rate. This is the real cost of repaying credit. Methods of calculation vary, but the result is the actual cost over one year of a loan incurring interest in (e.g.) monthly instalments.

Arab names Transliteration of Arab names will always lead to anomalies.

House styles vary but usually it is better to end Arab names in *i* rather than *y* (*Ali* not *Aly*, *Gaddafi* not *Gaddafy*).

The words *al* and *el* both mean *the*. They should be in lower case and followed by a hyphen. *Al-* is more common but use *el-* if that is how the person spells his or her name in English.

In personal names starting with *al-* or *el-* include the particle only at first reference, e.g. *Syrian President Hafez al-Assad* at first reference, thereafter *Assad*. In place and other names the particle is retained at second reference, e.g. *al-Arish*, (*the newspaper*) *al-Akhbar*.

Particles that go in lower case are *ait* (*Mohamed ait Atta*), *bin* and *bint* (*Aziza bint Ahmed*), *ibn* (*Abdulaziz ibn Sultan*), *ben* (*Ahmed ben Bella*), *bar*, *bou* and *ould* (*Moktar ould Daddah*).

Always use *bin*, not *ibn*, for *son of*, e.g. *Prince Sultan bin Abdul-Aziz*.

Retain the title *sheikh* at second reference, when the first name after the title is used, e.g. *Sheikh Ali al-Khalifa al-Sabah*, then *Sheikh Ali*.

See also **capitalisation, royalty**.

Arabian Gulf See **Gulf**.

Aramco See **Saudi Aramco**.

archaeology Not *archeology*.

Argentina, Argentine Not *the Argentine* as a noun or *Argentinian* as an adjective.

aristocratic titles Capitalise when they accompany a personal name; otherwise use lower case, e.g. *the Duke of Edinburgh, the Marquis of Bath*, but *the duke, the marquis*. Note that British dukes, earls, marquises, viscounts, barons and life peers are referred to collectively as peers not lords.

See also **nobility.**

artificial intelligence A discipline which aims to make machines reason like humans. In practice it works by giving computers an elaborate set of rules, known as knowledge engineering.

as   Often overused, especially in linking two developments that may have only a distant connection and may occur in different time frames, e.g. *Saddam issued new threats against Israel as Bush mulled his options in the Middle East.* Use with restraint, preferably when actions are both contemporaneous and closely linked, e.g. *Smith leaped out of the window as Jones kicked down the door.* Instead, use the word *and* or make it two sentences.

as, like   *As* compares verbs, *like* compares nouns. *He acted as a hero should* but *He acted like a hero.*

ASCII   The American standard code for information interchange. This assigns a binary number to each alphanumeric character. By using more pulses it provides for upper and lower case and other characters not available in Baudot (**q.v.**). It is sometimes called seven-level or eight-level code.

ASEAN   Association of Southeast Asian Nations. Its six members in 1992: Brunei, Indonesia, Malaysia, the Philippines, Singapore and Thailand.

Ashkenazim   Jews of East or Central European descent as opposed to Sephardim who are Jews of Spanish or Portuguese descent. Adjectives *Ashkenazic, Sephardic.*

Asiatic   Use *Asian.*

Assam   The northeastern state of Assam, one of India's main tea and oil-producing states, faces two revolts. The leftist United Liberation Front of Assam (ULFA) is fighting a decade-old campaign for an independent, socialist state. Its main targets are officials and security forces and tea planters, many of whom fled in 1990. Bodo tribesmen are fighting for their own state within India.

assure, reassure   See **reassure.**

astronomical names   Capitalise the names of heavenly bodies, e.g. *Betelgeuse, the Great Bear, Jupiter.* Capitalise *Sun, Moon,* and *Earth* when listing them among the planets but not in other references. Capitalise earth in phrases like *Mother Earth* or *Planet Earth.*

asynchronous   A communications method in which data is sent as soon as it is ready.

attempt   *Try* is shorter, better.

Auschwitz   Polish and Jewish experts have revised from the earlier widely accepted figure of four million to about 1.5 million the number of people, mainly Jews, killed by the Germans in the death camp at Auschwitz, southern Poland, during World War Two. Most of the killings actually took place in Birkenau, a satellite camp of Auschwitz. The Polish name is Oswiecim.

author   As a verb use *write*.

automatic   See **weapons**.

AWACS   airborne warning and control system, or an aircraft that carries such a system.

azimuth   Direction, or angle in the horizontal plane, e.g. for pointing a dish at a satellite.

B

Baath Rival wings of the Arab Baath Socialist Party ruled Iraq and Syria (in 1992). The short form Baath Party is acceptable. Baath means renaissance.

background Background is essential to the understanding of any story of substance. It should be woven seamlessly into the fabric of a story, not inserted in large blocks. Sometimes it should be in the lead, as in this example: *Armenia, which suffered a devastating earthquake in 1988, wants seismologists around the world to. . . .* A simple declarative sentence high in a story can be an effective way of providing background.

Baha'i An adherent of a religion founded by the 19th-century Persian prophet Baha-ullah. Note apostrophe.

Bahamas A native of the Bahamas is a *Bahamian* not a *Bahaman*.

bail, bale You *bail* out a boat or a company in difficulties but *bale* out of an aircraft.

balk Not *baulk*.

ballot *balloted*.

bandwidth This defines the range of frequencies that can safely be carried on a communications channel. A narrow band circuit can carry only low-frequency signals. Radio or television transmission requires broad bandwidth.

bank rate This is called discount rate in many countries, notably the U.S., Germany and Japan. In the U.K. it is known as the minimum lending rate (MLR). It is the interest rate at which a central bank will discount government paper or lend money against government paper collateral. Refer to it as *bank rate* not *the bank rate*.
See also **discount rate**.

bankruptcy A company becomes formally bankrupt or insolvent when a court rules it is unable to meet its debts. The ruling may be sought either by the company concerned (voluntary liquidation) or by creditors. In England the court appoints an official receiver to manage and eventually realise the debtor's assets on behalf of the creditors.

Terms like bankruptcy, insolvency and liquidation have different legal meanings in different countries. Be as precise as possible in reporting what a company or court says, especially if a translation is involved. For example, in France the normal form of bankruptcy is *faillite*; the term *banqueroute* refers to fraudulent bankruptcy. The danger if they are confused is obvious.

Similarly in Germany a collapse known as *Bankrott* is more serious than a normal liquidation. In the United States a company making a Chapter 11 (**q.v.**) application seeks protection from its creditors, not the winding up of its business.

Applications made under bankruptcy rules may be technical manoeuvres and could lead to libel actions if misinterpreted.

Business collapses are often progressive rather than sudden. Over-colourful reporting that implies the situation is hopeless may lead to legal trouble if the company recovers and claims the reports were false and damaging.

Reporters should keep for at least two years notes and tapes on which they have based a story that might be legally sensitive.

base rate   The annual interest rate on which graduated lending charges are calculated by British banks. Also called *reference rate* in Australia and *prime rate* (**q.v.**) in the United States.

basically   In nine cases out of 10 a word that can be cut from a story without any loss of sense.

Basle   Not *Basel* or *Bale*, Switzerland.

Basques   Guerrillas of the ETA (Euskadi Ta Askatasuna – Basque Homeland and Freedom) have been fighting since 1968 for full independence from Madrid for the Basque country. Made up of the northeastern provinces of Vizcaya, Guipuzcoa and Alava, this is one of Spain's 17 autonomous regions. More than 600 people had been killed up to 1990. Herri Batasuna (People's Unity) is the only party that supports the methods of ETA and is referred to as ETA's political arm. ETA has some support from the French Basque country across the Pyrenees.

Basra   Not *Basrah*, Iraq.

battalion   Not *batallion*.

battledress   One word. This is a uniform. If referring to soldiers wearing ammunition pouches, entrenching tools and other fighting equipment write *troops in battle gear* not *in battledress*.

baud   Pulses per second, used to express the rating of equipment of circuitry in a communications system. Named after Emile Baudot, a pioneer in data transmission.

Baudot   A data-transmission code in which five bits represent one character. It cannot support upper and lower case.

baulk   Use *balk*.

bayonet   *bayoneted*.

Beaufort Scale   See **storms**.

BBC   British Broadcasting Corporation. The initials alone may be used in the U.K. Otherwise it is better to give the full name at first reference.

bed and breakfast   The practice of selling shares and immediately buying them back at the end of a tax year to establish a gain or a loss for capital gains tax purposes.

bedouin   A desert Arab. Same in singular and plural.

Beijing   Frequently used in preference to *Peking*, China.

Beijing massacre   China's Communist leadership ended seven weeks of nationwide pro-democracy and anti-government demonstrations in 1989 by ordering thousands of troops backed by tanks to crush protests in Beijing on the night of June 4. An exact death toll was never made public. The government said more than 200 civilians and dozens of soldiers were killed. Human rights organisations, diplomats and foreign reporters estimated that between 1,000 and 3,000 people died. Although central Beijing's Tiananmen Square was the centre of the protest, the June 4 events should not be called the Tiananmen Square massacre, as many of the dead were killed outside the square.

Belarus   Not *Byelorussia* or *Belorussia*.

Bell modem   The U.S. standard modem (**q.v.**).

benefit   *benefited*.

Benelux The Benelux countries are Belgium, the Netherlands and Luxembourg.

beriberi A disease caused by vitamin deficiency. One word.

besiege Not *beseige*.

between, among See **among, between.**

bhang See **drugs – marijuana**.

bias *biased*.

biannual, biennial It's clearer to write *twice yearly, every two years.*

biblical Not *Biblical*.

billion One thousand million. The word should be spelled out. When reporting a range of figures use the style *1.2 billion to 1.4 billion* not *1.2–1.4 billion*.
 See also **figures, trillion.**

binary A number system with only two digits, 0 and 1, or any system that has only two possible states or levels, e.g. on/off.

bit A binary digit; it has one of only two values, 0 or 1. It is the smallest unit of data recognised by a computer. Data handled by computer is digitised, or expressed as a combination of bits, often expressed as kilobits or megabits.
 See **units of measurement** in Appendix II – Technical Glossary.

biweekly This can mean twice a week or once every two weeks. So avoid it.

black Acceptable as noun or adjective as a synonym for Negro but not for coloured (**q.v.**).

Black Africa See **Africa.**

black box Popular term for aircraft recording equipment. Although they are not in fact black, the term may be used if it is made clear that the reference is to a plane's flight recorder or its flight-deck voice recorder.

blind Describe people as blind only if they are totally without sight. Otherwise write that *their sight is impaired* or that they have *only partial vision.*

blitzkrieg   German for lightning war or violent attack. Use the short form *blitz* only for heavy air attacks.

blond, blonde   When used as nouns, *blond* for a man, *blonde* for a woman. But the adjective is always *blond*.

B'nai B'rith   A Jewish service and community organisation. Note apostrophes.

boat people   In 1991 there were about 127,000 Vietnamese boat people in camps around Asia, the largest number being in Hong Kong where of about 64,000 inmates only 5,000 had been classified as bona fide refugees eligible to settle in the West rather than as so-called economic migrants. Other countries with big populations included Indonesia (20,000), Thailand (15,000), Philippines (13,500) and Malaysia (13,500). Japan, South Korea, Macau and Singapore also had small populations.

In 1989 a Comprehensive Plan of Action (CPA) aimed at solving the problem was signed by Vietnam, Britain, the ASEAN (**q.v.**) nations and major resettlement countries including the United States, Australia, Canada, and France.

The CPA includes a screening system and a programme for boat people to return home voluntarily. By October 1991 almost 11,000 people had returned home voluntarily from Hong Kong but this figure has been far outstripped by new arrivals in the meantime.

Under the CPA, Vietnam committed itself to speeding up the Orderly Departure Programme under which officials of the former South Vietnamese regime can leave the country legally for resettlement elsewhere. Hanoi has also guaranteed that boat people returning home will not be persecuted.

Forced repatriation was tried in Hong Kong in December 1989, when 51 people were deported. After an international outcry, particularly in the United States, Vietnam vetoed further forced repatriations. Vietnam is sensitive to U.S. reaction as it is trying to mend relations with Washington as a key part of a drive to end its international isolation. But in October 1991 Vietnam and Hong Kong agreed to resume forced repatriation.

bogey, bogie   *Bogey* is a golf term, meaning one stroke above par for a hole. A *bogie* is a trolley.

book titles   House styles vary but usually one puts book titles (but not those of newspapers or magazines) in italics or inside quotation marks. Exceptions are major reference works and very well-known books such as the Bible, the Koran, the Oxford English Dictionary. Capitalise every word in the title apart from conjunctions, articles, particles and short prepositions, e.g. *"The Rise and Fall of the Third Reich"*.

both *Both sides agreed* is tautology. Write *The two sides agreed*.

Bosphorus Not *Bosphorous*. The Turkish waterway separating Europe from Asia and linking the Black Sea with the Aegean and the Mediterranean.

boss This word has pejorative or slang connotations and, headlines apart, should not be used in serious contexts, e.g. *A Mitterrand aide said his boss. . . .* However, *Mafia bosses* would be permissible and the word can be used in an informal context, e.g. *Betty Smith said she was sick of correcting her boss's spelling*.

boycott The refusal of a group to deal with a person or use a commodity. An embargo is a legal ban on trade.

bps bits (**q.v.**) per second, a measure of transmission speed, often expressed as Kbps or Mbps (kilo-, megabits).

brackets If an entire sentence is in brackets, put the full stop inside the closing bracket, e.g. *. . . reported earlier.*)
   If a sentence has a bracketed section at the end, the full stop goes outside the closing bracket, e.g. *. . . reported earlier*). If a bracketed section in the middle of a sentence is followed by a comma, that also goes outside the bracket.

brand names See **trademarks.**

Britain Do not use England as a synonym for Britain or the United Kingdom. Britain comprises England, Scotland and Wales. The United Kingdom comprises Britain and Northern Ireland. Normally use Britain unless the Irish context is important.

British Isles A geographical, not political term. They comprise the United Kingdom, islands under the British Crown such as the Channel Islands and Isle of Man, and the Republic of Ireland. See also **Britain, U.K.**

broken quotes A profusion of quotation marks around unremarkable parts of sentences and single words breaks the flow of a sentence and irritates the reader. A word or phrase should be quoted only if it has a special resonance or if you need to make clear that the choice of words is not yours but that of your source. It is better to quote one or more full sentences, shortening them if necessary by omitting words, e.g. *"We will fight . . . and we will win."* Some examples of misuse:

> *Bush said he was "happy" to be in France.*
> *Bhutto said the elections had been "rigged".*

Legitimate use of broken quotes:

> *Olivier's widow said a "huge wave of love" had engulfed the family.*
> *Bhutto said the elections had been rigged in a "disgusting travesty of the democratic process".*

See also **quotation**.

budget   *budgeted.*

buffalo   *buffaloes.*

buildup   One word as a noun, two as a verb and adverb.

bulletin   The term used by some news agencies to designate their top-priority stories. A bulletin is very short but should be properly sourced. See also **flash, urgent**.

bureau   *bureaux.*

burgeoning   An overused (and often incorrectly used) adjective. *Burgeoning* means *putting forth shoots* or *beginning to grow rapidly.* If you just mean growing, say so.

Burma   The Rangoon government has renamed the country Myanmar but the old name is almost universally used.

Burmese names   Keep the full name at second reference. *U* means *Mr* and *Daw* means *Mrs.* When *U* is followed by a single name it should be retained, e.g. *U Nu.*

bus   Plural buses, present participle busing. *Passenger bus* is tautologous.

business abbreviations   See Appendix III for a list of abbreviations commonly used in business stories.

by   As a prefix needs no hyphen, except in *by-election, by-law, by-product.*

Byelorussia   See **Belarus**.

bylines   A byline – the name of the writer – should be used only on non-routine stories of substance.

byte   The number of bits used to represent a character, usually eight, sometimes seven. Kilobytes and megabytes, rather than kilobits and megabits, are used to measure data storage capacity.

See **units of measurement** in Appendix II – Technical Glossary.

C

cablese   A compressed form of writing formerly used to save costs when messages were filed by cable. News agencies still use cablese in service messages from habit rather than necessity, e.g. *fyi white house downplaying likelihood bush bonnwarding enroute moscow summit*. Never use such words in copy.

caffeine   Not *caffein*.

calibre   See **weapons**.

Cambodia   Use this form rather than *Kampuchea*, unless directly quoting. Full names should be used at all references except in the case of royalty. *Prince Norodom Sihanouk* becomes *Sihanouk* at second reference.

The radical, Maoist Khmer Rouge, backed by China, took over Cambodia in 1975 and began a reign of terror in which it killed more than a million people. Vietnam, traditionally hostile to China, invaded Cambodia late in 1978 and drove out the Khmer Rouge, installing a pro-Hanoi government in its place. The Khmer Rouge then became the dominant force in a loose anti-government guerrilla alliance with two non-Communist groups, the Khmer People's National Liberation Front (KPNLF), whose leader is former prime minister Son Sann, and the Sihanoukists, directly loyal to the former ruler, Prince Norodom Sihanouk, who was also titular leader of the alliance.

The three guerrilla factions and the Phnom Penh government signed a United Nations-brokered peace treaty in Paris in 1991, formally ending 13 years of civil war. Under the plan a reconciliation body, the Supreme National Council headed by Sihanouk, would embody Cambodian sovereignty until free U.N.-supervised elections, expected to be held some time in 1993, for a 120-seat national assembly.

U.N. peacekeepers began arriving in Phnom Penh in November 1991 to oversee a ceasefire and disarmament of the factions. UNTAC, the United Nations Transitional Authority in Cambodia, is charged with maintaining peace in Cambodia and supervising the elections.

Cameroon   Not *Cameroun* or *the Cameroons*, West Africa.

can   Do not confuse with *may*. *You can do this* means you are able to do it. *You may do this* means that you are permitted to do it.

cancer   See **medical stories** on the need for caution in handling stories about reputed cures for cancer.

canister   Not *cannister*.

cannon, canon   A *cannon* is a large-calibre gun (same singular and plural), a *canon* a law or a church dignitary.

Canterbury, Archbishop of   See **Anglican Church.**

canvas, canvass   You paint on a *canvas* but *canvass* for votes.

capable, capability   Use with restraint. Write *The aircraft can carry 300 passengers* not *The aircraft is capable of carrying 300 passengers*. Likewise *The U.S. can launch. . . .* not *The U.S. has the capability to launch. . . .*

capital   Write, e.g. *the Syrian capital, Damascus*, not *the Syrian capital of Damascus*.

capitalisation   Putting the first letter of a word in capitals makes it more limited and specific, e.g. *He was a Communist with conservative instincts.* There are no rigid rules on capitalisation and house styles vary widely. In the absence of a specific house ruling, the following guidance for Reuter journalists may be helpful. When in doubt it is better to avoid the capital.

Abbreviations: They normally follow the capitalisation of the unabbreviated form, e.g. *European currency unit, Ecu; miles per hour, mph; Western European Union, WEU.*

Academic, aristocratic, military and religious titles: Capitalise when they accompany a personal name, otherwise use lower case, e.g. *Professor John Smith, Admiral Horatio Nelson* but *the history professor, the admiral.*

Acronyms: When an acronym is made up of initial letters that are themselves capitalised, then capitalise each letter, e.g. *NATO* for the *North Atlantic Treaty Organisation.* But if the acronym is formed from initial syllables rather than letters, then capitalise only the first letter, e.g. *Aramco* for *Arabian American Oil Company.*

Armed forces: Normally use lower case for the armed services, e.g. *U.S. army, British navy, French air force.* Capitalise such specific names as *the Royal Air Force, the Royal Canadian Navy* and *the (German) Bundeswehr, Luftwaffe* and in a historical context *Wehrmacht.*

Astronomical: Capitalise the names of heavenly bodies, e.g. *Betelgeuse, the Great Bear, Jupiter,* but not *the sun, moon, and earth* (except in a phrase like *Mother Earth* or *Planet Earth* or when listing *Earth* among the planets).

Colons: Colons are followed by lower case unless the next word is a proper name, a direct quotation or the beginning of a sentence.

Corporate/organisational titles: Do not capitalise titles like *PLO chairman Yasser Arafat* or *Super-Widgets Plc managing director Peter Brown.*

Dashes: Dashes (–) are followed by lower case unless they are used to label sections of a list, e.g.

The study concluded:

– Almost half had more exports this year than last.

– In 1991, a third had less imports than in 1990.

– One in five expects better terms of trade in 1993.

Geographical and geological names: Capitalise these, apart from particles, articles, and compass references not forming part of the proper name, e.g. *the River Plate* but *the river; North Korea* but *north London; Nile Delta* but *the delta of the Nile;* the *Upper Pleistocene;* the *Lower East Side of New York* but *the lower east bank of the river.*

Geopolitical: Capitalise nouns and adjectives which have a geographic origin but are used politically, e.g. *Western influence, the North-South divide, the West, Eastern Europe.*

Government ministers: Capitalise the title at first reference when it precedes the full name. When the title follows the name or is used alone, use lower case, e.g.: *French Foreign Minister Roland Dumas; Roland Dumas, the French foreign minister; the foreign minister. President George Bush* but *The president said. . . .*

Governmental bodies: Treat governmental bodies as proper names, capitalising them when an integral part of a specific name but not when unspecific as in plurals or standing alone, e.g. *the Israeli Foreign Ministry* or *The Foreign Ministry said Israel would.* . . . But *The ministry added* . . .; *the Australian Parliament* but *the Australian and New Zealand parliaments*; likewise *the EC Executive Commission* but *the commission.* However refer to the European Community as *the Community* at second reference.

Hyphenated titles: When a hyphenated title is capitalised, capitalise both parts, e.g. *Lieutenant-General John Smith, Secretary-General Javier Perez de Cuellar.*

Legislative bodies: Capitalise the names of legislative bodies (*Parliament, Senate, the Diet*) at all references. The one exception is when they are used in the plural, e.g. *The Norwegian and Danish parliaments.* . . .

Nationality and race: Capitalise words denominating nationality, race or language, e.g. *Arab, African, Argentine, Caucasian, Chinese, Eskimo, Finnish.*

Nicknames: Treat them as proper names when they refer to a specific person or thing, e.g. *the Iron Lady, the All Blacks, the Bermuda Triangle.*

Politics: Capitalise the names of political parties and of movements with a specific doctrine, e.g. *a Communist official, a Democratic senator.* Use lower case for non-specific references, e.g. *the settlement was run on communist principles, he proposed a democratic vote.*

Proper names: Common nouns that normally have no initial capital are capitalised when they are an integral part of the full name of a person, organisation or thing, e.g. *Queen Elizabeth, the Sultan of Brunei, President Hosni Mubarak, General John Smith, Senator Jack Brown, the River Thames, Christian Democratic Party, the Church Assembly.*

These nouns are normally lower case if they stand alone or in the plural or refer to a title no longer current, e.g. *former president Jimmy Carter, the queen, the Malaysian sultan, down the river, Christian Democratic parties.*

It is better to break this rule, however, than to risk ambiguity, e.g. *The Speaker told the House of Commons* . . . Retain the capital also when the person remains specific because there is only one or he or she is pre-eminent, e.g. *the Dalai Lama, the Pontiff, the Pope, the Virgin (Mary).*

Proper nouns: Capitalise words that uniquely identify a particular person or thing, e.g. *John Smith, General Motors, Mount Everest.*

Exceptions here are for articles and particles used as auxiliaries in names like *Robert the Bruce, Charles de Gaulle.*

Keep the capital on words that derive their meaning from a proper noun, e.g. *Americanise, Christian, Marxist, Shakespearian, Stalinist.*

Do not keep it when the connection with the proper noun is remote, e.g. *arabic numerals, boycott, chauvinistic, french polish, herculean, pasteurise.*

Publications: Whatever the masthead says, do not capitalise articles and particles in the names of newspapers and magazines, e.g. *the New York Times, the News of the World.*

For books, films, plays, poems, operas, songs and works of art capitalise every word in the title apart from conjunctions, articles, particles and short prepositions, e.g. *The Rise and Fall of the Third Reich, The Merchant of Venice, Gone with the Wind.*

Quotes: A statement that follows a colon quote begins with a capital, e.g. "Guzhenko said: 'The conference has ignored the principle of equality'."

Religion: Names of divinities are capitalised but unspecific plurals are lower case, e.g. *Allah, the Almighty, Christ, God, Jehovah, the Deity, the Holy Trinity, Zeus* but *the gods, the lords of the universe.*

Capitalise names of denominations and religious movements, e.g. *Baptist, Buddhist, Christian, Church of England, Islamic, Jew, Jewish, Moslem, Orthodox.* But non-denominational references are lower case, e.g. *adult baptism, orthodox beliefs, built a temple.* The Pope is head of *the Roman Catholic Church* or of *the Church* (that is, the whole body of Roman Catholics) but he would celebrate mass in a Roman Catholic church (that is, a building).

Sentences: The first word of a sentence is always capitalised, unless it is contained within brackets as part of another sentence (this is an example). Capitalise the particle of a family name at the start of a sentence, e.g. *Van den Boeynants said. . . .*

Sports: Treat specific events as proper names, general references as common nouns, e.g. *the Olympic Games, the Belgian Grand Prix,* but *an athletics meeting, a motor racing championship.*

Transport: Names of aircraft, cars, trains and ships are capitalised, e.g. *the Cutty Sark, USS Forrestal,* a *Nimrod,* a *Nissan Primera, the Orient Express.*

captions   Picture captions should meet a newspaper's standards of accuracy, objectivity and simplicity of language.

Never write a caption without seeing the picture it describes. The caption must make clear what is happening in the picture without wasting words describing what is evident from the picture itself, in language that is crisp, easy to read and free from unnecessary adjectives, cuteness, slang, parochialism and editorialising.

Everyone significant in the picture must be identified. This means giving a name or, for example, identifying a masked figure as *the IRA gunman.* If there is a name, ensure it is attributed to the right person in the picture, correctly spelt and in house style – for example *former Chancellor Willy Brandt* not *Socialist boss Herr Brandt.* People should be named from left to right where possible.

The caption must leave no doubt about when and where the picture was taken. Use the date, e.g. *President Bush addressed Congress on January 25,* etc. If there is any doubt about the location of a picture spell it out precisely, e.g. *at Bedford, 60 miles*

(95 km) north of London, but do not include unnecessary local detail.

carbine A short-barrelled rifle.

careen, career You *careen* a ship by turning it on its side to clean the hull. To *career* is to move rapidly.

cargo *cargoes.*

carrier Use only in reference to aircraft carriers, i.e. ships from which fixed-wing aircraft can take off. Helicopter carriers should be referred to by the full name.

cartridge In describing the scene of a gun fight distinguish between bullets (the projectiles fired) and the spent cartridge cases (which contained the propellant charge). The cartridge comprises a metal cartridge case, a priming charge, the propellant and the bullet.

casino *casinos.*

CATV cable television.

caution As a verb prefer *warn* except in the usage *Police cautioned the man before he made a statement*. Do not write, for instance, *He cautioned that war was imminent.*

CBI Confederation of British Industry.

CCITT The Comité Consultatif International de Télégraphique et Téléphonique (of the International Telecommunication Union (ITU)). Agrees on standards and protocols for international communications, known as "recommendations". The term is also used to distinguish the international news pictures transmission standard from the domestic U.S. standard.

CCITT modem International standard modem.

CDU Christian Democratic Union (West Germany).

ceasefire One word as a noun. The verb form is *to cease fire.*

cello *cellos.*

Celsius See **temperatures**.

Centigrade   Increasingly the media are using *Celsius* instead of *Centigrade* to refer to the scale of temperatures.

centimetre   Abbreviation *cm* (no full stop, same singular and plural), acceptable at all references. To convert to inches roughly multiply by 2 and divide by 5, to convert precisely multiply by 0.394.

centre   You centre *on* something not *(a)round* it.

CFE   Conventional Forces in Europe. Talks, which began in Vienna in 1989 between the NATO and Warsaw Pact states (**q.v.**), under the auspices of the Conference on Security and Cooperation in Europe (CSCE). A treaty signed in Paris in November 1990 provided for major cuts in tanks, armoured vehicles, artillery, aircraft and helicopters deployed in Europe between the Atlantic and the Urals. Follow-up talks are focusing on reducing troop levels in the same area.

channel   *channelled.*

Chapter 11   Under this aspect of U.S. bankruptcy laws a debtor, unable to pay his debts, remains in possession of his business and in control of its operations, unless a court rules otherwise. Chapter 11 gives debtors and creditors considerable flexibility in working together to reorganise the business. See also **bankruptcy**.

charisma   A grossly overused vogue word which now means little more than *personal charm*. Use it with discrimination of people (other than rock stars and the like) who have a capacity to inspire devotion among their followers.

check, cheque   A restaurant bill is a *check*, a money order a *cheque*.

Chinaman   This term is considered offensive. Use *Chinese man*.

Chinese names   Although the pinyin phonetic alphabet is generally used for the translation of Chinese words into Roman script, most media organisations still use the old form for the following names:
   Canton, China, Inner Mongolia (and its capital *Hohhot*), *Kashgar, Khotan, Tibet* (and its cities of *Lhasa* and *Shigatse*), *Urumqi; Chou Enlai, Mao Tsetung, Sun Yatsen;* and Tibetan names like *the Panchen Lama*.
   Mainland Chinese do not hyphenate the given name, e.g. *Deng Xiaoping*. Taiwan Chinese do, with the second part in lower case, e.g. *Chiang Ching-kuo*.

In both cases use only the surname at second reference, e.g. *Deng, Chiang*.

Church of England   See **Anglican Church.**

Church of Scotland   Although the established church in Scotland, the Church of Scotland, unlike the Church of England, recognises no head. Its senior representative, chosen annually, is the Moderator of the General Assembly of the Church of Scotland. Do not shorten to Moderator of the Church of Scotland.

CIA   Central Intelligence Agency (U.S.). The initials may be used alone as an adjective in a lead paragraph if it is clear from the context what is meant.

circumlocution   Speakers who confuse length with profundity are only too prone to use long-winded phraseology. Journalists are under no obligation to follow their example. Occasionally, if it occurs in a key quotation, you have to retain a circumlocution, e.g. *The president said: "At this moment in time our bombers are heading for the Ruritanian capital."* In general, however, you should turn into indirect speech and decent prose the rhetorical flourishes of the pompous. Some locutions are so common that they tend to slip past any but the most vigilant sub-editor, e.g.:

adjacent to	next to
prior to	before
as a result of	because of
got under way	began
in consequence of	because of
in order to	to
in the first instance	first
owing to the fact that	because
he himself	he
end result	result
at the side of	beside
each and every	every
horns of a dilemma	dilemma
pre-planned	planned
weather conditions	weather
went to the polls	voted

has the capability of	can
conducted a search operation	searched

See also **euphemism, long words**.

claimed   Use of this word suggests that the writer does not believe the statement in question. Prefer *said*. However, it is acceptable to say that a guerrilla organisation *claimed responsibility* for carrying out an attack. Do not say that it *claimed credit*.

cliches   News stories relying heavily on phrases that have become stale through overuse are like paintings done by number. They convey information but lack life or freshness. Avoid cliches, particularly those that exaggerate or over-simplify, e.g. *the postage stamp-sized country, the oil-rich sheikhdom.*

There is a place for the occasional cliche, when no more graphic, simple alternative comes to mind and the phrase is genuinely applicable to the situation being described. For example the cliche *up to his eyes in* seems legitimate in *Smith was already up to his eyes in work when the avalanche of forms landed on his desk* since it conjures up a graphic impression of a man deluged in paper.

Again, use of a cliche is more acceptable when it is done with a sense of humour or irony, e.g. in a story on a company in deep trouble: *The writing is on the wall for blackboard manufacturers Brown and Copthorne.*

Some cliches to avoid:

In disasters: *mercy mission, airlifted/rushed to hospital, giant C-130 transports, massive aid, an air and sea search was under way, disaster probe, sifted through the wreckage.*

Of violence: *lone gunman, strife-torn province, embattled city, baton-wielding police, stone-throwing demonstrators, steel-helmeted troops braced themselves for, police swoop, staged an attack on,* (tautologically) *anti-government rebels.*

In diplomacy and politics: *face-to-face talks on key issues, top-level meeting, headed into talks on, spearheaded a major initiative, rubber-stamp parliament, lashed out, go to the polls, behind closed doors.*

Of industrial trouble: *top union leaders, industrial action, bosses, in a bid to settle, braced themselves for.*

See also **jargon**.

cocaine   See **drugs**.

COCOM   Coordinating Committee for Multilateral Export Controls. Established in 1949, COCOM currently (1992) has 17 members – Japan, Australia and all NATO (**q.v.**) states except Iceland. Its purpose is to prevent technology that could have military uses from falling through trade into the hands of Communist countries. It maintains a Security Export Control list of items. This was greatly liberalised in June 1990, following East European moves to democracy. COCOM operates by informal agreement and has a secretariat in Paris.

collective nouns   House styles vary but usually collective nouns and names of countries, governments, organisations and companies are followed by singular verbs and singular neuter pronouns, e.g. *The government, which is studying the problem, said it* . . . not *The government, who are studying the problem, said they.* . . .

collision   Beware of the legal danger of imputing blame in a collision. But avoid clumsy phraseology like *The Danish freighter was in collision with the German tanker.* Better to write *The Danish freighter and the German tanker collided.*
    Only two moving objects can collide. It is wrong therefore to write *The ferry collided with the jetty. Hit* is enough.

colons   See **punctuation.**

colour separations   A means of transmitting a colour picture by breaking it down into three components, referred to as cyan, magenta and yellow (from the inks used to print it). Sometimes a fourth element, black, is added.

coloured   Use of people only in the context of South Africa, where it is an official classification for a person of mixed race. The story should make this clear. Lower case. See also **race.**

commando   *commandos.*

commas   See **punctuation.**

commence   *Begin* is usually better.

comment   See **interpretation.**

commit   Past tense *committed*, noun *commitment.*

Commonwealth of Independent States   The Soviet Union ceased to exist at the end of 1991, when the Commonwealth of Independent States (CIS) was formed. Its 11 members at the beginning of 1992 were Armenia, Azerbaijan, Belarus, Kazakhstan, Kyrgyzstan,

Moldova, Russia, Tajikistan, Turkmenistan, Ukraine, Uzbekistan. (Styles vary but these are the approved Reuter spellings.) Georgia and the newly independent Baltic republics, Estonia, Latvia and Lithuania, were not members of the commonwealth. Reuter style is to refer to the commonwealth by its full title at first reference. On second reference it is *the commonwealth* (with lower-case *c*).

See also **Soviet cities**.

communique   An official announcement. It is tautological to write *an official communique*. *Statement* is usually better.

Comoro Islands   Or simply *the Comoros* for the Indian Ocean group.

company names   When writing about a company give the full legal company name at some point (including Inc, Ltd, Plc, etc.), normally at first reference. This is because many companies in the same group often have similar names and it is only by giving the full names that a specialist can distinguish between them.

When giving the company's full name observe the spelling, capitalisation and punctuation used by the company.

Use the following abbreviations, without a full stop, to indicate the kind of registered company. When such abbreviations come at the end of a company name they are not preceded by a comma.

AB	Aktiebolaget
AG	Aktiengesellschaft
A/S	Aktieselskabet
Cie	Compagnie
Co	Company
Cos	Companies
Corp	Corporation
GmbH	Gesellschaft mit beschaenkter Haftung
Inc	Incorporated
KK	Kabushiki Kaisha
Ltd	Limited
Plc	Public limited company
SpA	Società per Azioni

comparisons   Be sure that you are comparing like with like. It is wrong to write *The food situation was not so bad as the near-famine years* or *The weapon's range was twice as great as the Kalashnikov*. You cannot compare a situation with years or a distance with a weapon.

Write *The food situation was not so bad as that in the near-famine years* or *The weapon's range was twice as great as the Kalashnikov's.*

Special care is needed with statistical comparisons. One month may not be comparable with another because of its length or the number of national holidays it contains. December figures for one country may not be comparable with another's because the countries are in different hemispheres.

compass points Capitalise compass points only when they form part of a proper name – *North Korea,* but *north London; the Lower East Side of New York,* but *the lower east bank of the river.*

Omit hyphens in the four basic compounds *northwest, northeast, southwest, southeast.* Use a hyphen in the minor compounds such as *north-northeast.*

You do not write *northern Connecticut* or *southern Kent* when you mean to say that Connecticut is a northern state or Kent a southern county. So do not say *northern Chiang Mai* or *eastern Kivu province.* It is the *northern town of Chiang Mai* or the *eastern province of Kivu.*

complement, compliment To *complement* is to complete or to provide a matching component to something, e.g. *The British submarines complemented the U.S. surface ships.* To *compliment* is to express praise, regard or respect.

comprise Use only when listing all the component parts of a whole. *Benelux comprises Belgium, the Netherlands and Luxembourg. The European Community includes Belgium, the Netherlands and Luxembourg.*

compound If you mean *to make worse,* say so.

Comsat Communications Satellite Corporation (Washington), a private U.S. corporation created by the authority of Congress. It represents the U.S. on Intelsat (**q.v.**) where it also has a management role.

concealing sources If, as is sometimes necessary, you use a pseudonym to cloak the identity of a source or the subject of a story, make clear in copy that you have done so, e.g. *Our guide Mohammad (a pseudonym used to conceal his identity) led us over desert tracks. . . .*

confrontation   Modish but vague word. Use more specific terms if possible, e.g. *war, clash, dispute, test of wills.*

consensus   Not *concensus*. *General consensus* is tautological as consensus means either unanimity or a general trend of opinion.

consul-general   Note hyphen. Likewise *consulate-general.*

contact   Acceptable as a verb but it is better to be specific if you can and say whether two people met or spoke by telephone or exchanged letters.

contempt of court   A story that could be held to interfere with the course of justice could give rise to an action for contempt of court. Danger areas include allegations that a judge or court may have been motivated by bias, comments on the likely guilt or innocence of an accused person (e.g. a reference to a man not yet convicted as *the murderer*), reporting while a trial is in progress of an accused's previous convictions or of information about the case not presented in court, disregarding reporting restrictions in court proceedings (e.g. in juvenile or rape cases), reporting that an accused person has confessed. Note that reporting of a court case abroad that might affect the trial in another country could constitute contempt. Under British law, however, any fair and accurate report of public legal proceedings that is published contemporaneously and in good faith is considered not to be in contempt of court.

Draw your editor's attention to any story that you think might possibly constitute contempt and explain your reservations.

Reporters should keep for at least two years notes and tapes on which they have based a story that might be legally sensitive.

continual, continuous   *Continual* means *frequent and repeated*, *continuous* means *uninterrupted.*

continued   Avoid the use of the verb *continued* in lead paragraphs. It implies a monotony not calculated to gain a reader's attention.

Contra   Formerly a right-wing guerrilla in Nicaragua. Capitalise and explain.

contract note   A document stating that a transaction, such as the buying of shares or units in a unit trust, has taken place.

contractions   Use words like *isn't, aren't, can't* only when quoting someone or in an informal context. Many editors would think it inappropriate to write *The prime minister can't make up his mind whether to raise taxes or cut government spending* but would be happy with *For Georgia peanut farmer Fred Jenkins it isn't a question of whether, but when, he will go bankrupt.*

conurbation Not a synonym for *an urban area.* It means an aggregation of towns, like the New York-Boston or Tokyo-Osaka corridors.

conversions Conversions are a fertile source of error. Double-check them all. If you make a conversion precisely using a calculator, make a rough backward check to make sure that you have not added or lost a zero.

The usual practice is to give the local unit in the country of origin first and then the conversion to another currency or system of measurement in brackets.

If a figure for speed, distance, weight, etc., is approximate, the conversion should also be approximate. Write a *2,000-lb (900-kg) bomb* not a *2,000-lb (907-kg) bomb.*

When abbreviating metric units use the singular form without a full stop, e.g. *kg* or *km* not *kgs* or *kms.*

Do not give a conversion to more decimal places than are given in the original figure.

Do not convert the nautical mile used for fishing limits, by ships when reporting distances at sea and by NASA and others reporting space shots. If using nautical miles in space stories you should make this clear.

For metric to imperial conversions and vice versa see under the appropriate term, e.g. **gallon, metre, tonne.**

For temperature conversions, see **temperatures**.

See also **Ecu, measures, ton/tonne** and Appendix I – Conversions.

convince, persuade You *convince* people of something, *persuade* them to do something. You do not *convince* someone to do something.

court martial *courts martial.* The verb is *court-martial.*

courtesy titles House styles vary on whether or not to use courtesy titles such as *Mr, Mrs, Ms* or *Miss* or their foreign equivalents. Where they are not used, an exception should be made in a story about two persons with the same family name when you might refer for instance to *Mr Smith* and *Mrs Smith* to avoid confusion. You should also use at first reference titles of nobility and military, medical and religious titles, e.g. *Lord Ferrars, General Colin Powell, Dr Christiaan Barnard, the Rev. Jesse Jackson.*

See also **nobility, religious titles, royalty.**

crack   See **drugs.**

Cracow   Use *Krakow*, Poland.

credibility, creditworthiness   If you have the first you are likely to be believed, if the second you are likely to get a loan.

crescendo   A gradual increase in loudness. It is wrong to write that something *reached a crescendo.*

cricket   While this guide does not set out to cover sport, an entry on cricket is given because it is a sport peculiar to a small number of mainly Commonwealth countries which journalists of all nationalities may be asked to handle at some time.

Cricket is played between two teams of 11 players, the object being for one side to score more runs overall than their opponents.

Matches are played over two innings per side or, in one-day games, over one innings per side with a specified, equal number of overs (an over being six balls) for each team, the number varying according to the competition.

Captains toss a coin to determine who bats first. There are always two batsmen at the wickets, one who faces the bowling and one, called a non-striker, at the opposite end.

Runs are scored by the batsman who faces the bowling and he literally runs from one wicket to the other for each run. Hits along the ground that reach the boundary are worth four and hits over the boundary without touching the field count six.

When an odd number of runs is scored, usually one or three, it brings the non-striker to face the bowling.

The bowler bowls at one wicket for one over and then another bowler bowls from the opposite end for the same number of deliveries. Bowlers may be used for any length of time, except in one-day matches when they are restricted to a set number of overs each.

When 10 of the batsmen in a side have been dismissed, with the remaining player designated as not out by virtue of having no other batsman to partner him, the team's innings is ended and the other side bats.

After team A and team B have each batted once, team A start their second innings. (Team B could be asked to bat again immediately – "follow on" – if they were more than a specified number of runs behind team A.) The total runs scored by team A in their two innings must be exceeded by team B to win the game.

Thus, if team A score 100 runs in their first innings and 150 in the second, they have an aggregate of 250. If team B score 120 in their first innings they need 131 in their second innings for an aggregate of 251 which would make them match winners. A second-innings score of 130 all out would result in a tie.

In this sample scoreboard b = bowled, c = caught, st = stumped, lbw = leg before wicket, w = wide ball, lb = leg bye.

New Zealand

J.Wright b Fraser	9
R.Reid c Russell b Fraser	9
M.Crowe c Russell b Bicknell	5
A.Jones b Fraser	64
K.Rutherford c and b Tufnell	19
C.Harris st Russell b Tufnell	9
I.Smith lbw b Bicknell	28
C.Cairns c Smith b DeFreitas	5
G.Larsen not out	10
Pringle not out	18
Extras (w-11, lb-9)	20
Total (for eight wickets in 49 overs)	196

Did not bat: W.Watson.

Fall of wickets: 1-20 2-25 3-43 4-91 5-109 6-150 7-158 8-171

Bowling: Fraser 9-1-22-3 (w-1), Bicknell 10-0-65-2 (w-7), De-Freitas 10-2-22-1(w-1), Gooch 10-2-33-0 (w-2), Tufnell 10-0-45-2.

In the fall of wickets the total is listed when each batsman is dismissed. Thus, if an aggregate of 37 runs has been scored when the first batsman is out, it appears in the scoreboard as 1-37 and if the total is 66 when the next wicket falls it is 2-66.

In the bowling analysis 22-6-37-4, for example, means 22 overs have been bowled by the bowler in question, with six maidens (no runs conceded in each of those overs), a total of 37 runs have been scored off the bowlers, and he has taken four wickets.

A batsman is given out lbw (leg before wicket) if the ball hits his pads, preventing it, in the umpire's judgment, from hitting the wicket.

A leg bye is a run scored not from the bat but when the ball hits the batsman's pads and is not returned to the wicketkeeper by a fielder before the batsmen have completed a run.

criterion   Plural *criteria*.

cross rate   Any foreign exchange rate not including the dollar. Cross rates can be priced directly or through the dollar. In the latter case a trader who wants to sell sterling for marks, for example, would first sell sterling for dollars and then sell dollars for marks.

Cross rates are increasingly traded directly in the major currencies. But in less liquid cross currencies, such as, e.g., the Norwegian crown/Australian dollar cross, the deal would be channelled through the dollar.

crown   It is simpler to use this for the Nordic currencies than *kroner, kronor* or *kronur*.

crowd estimates   If the number of people involved in an event such as a demonstration or strike is at all controversial, the source should be given for the number quoted.

CRT   Cathode ray tube, commonly used in the U.S. as a synonym for a video display terminal.

CSCE   Conference on Security and Cooperation in Europe. In late 1991 it grouped the United States, Canada and all European states including the three Baltics. Other former Soviet republics were still represented by Moscow, and Yugoslavia represented Croatia and Slovenia. The CSCE held its first summit in Helsinki in 1975. This produced a "Final Act" detailing measures to improve military confidence, economic cooperation and human rights. Later conferences in Belgrade (1977–78), Madrid (1980–83) and Vienna (1986–89) elaborated on these measures. The Vienna meeting also launched the Conventional Forces in Europe (CFE) talks (**q.v.**). A Paris summit in November 1990 set up permanent institutions for the CSCE, which currently has 38 members. These were a secretariat in Prague, a conflict prevention centre in Vienna and an office for free elections in Warsaw.

CSU   Christian Social Union (Bavarian sister-party of the German CDU).

currency   Reports of currency devaluations and revaluations should give enough information to make the move understandable both to a specialist and to the man or woman in the street.

They should give both the old and the new rates against the dollar or the percentage devaluation or revaluation.

Announcements do not always express these changes in percentage terms. There are two ways to work out the percentage – domestic and international. The domestic calculation gives the percentage change in the exchange rate and is mainly of interest to people in the country concerned.

It is better to use the international calculation, which gives the effect of the currency change on the rest of the world. Business executives in particular want this, because it measures the extent by which a country's exports are being made more competitive (by devaluation) or less competitive (by revaluation).

The method of calculating percentage movements is: where the currency is expressed as so-many to the dollar, take the difference between the old and new rates, multiply by 100, and divide by the new rate, e.g.:

The Spanish peseta is devalued against the U.S. dollar. Old rate of 69.99 pesetas, subtracted from new rate of 87.40, leaves 17.41. Divide this by the new rate and multiply by 100 – result: 19.92 per cent. The initial report for the business services should be precise to four decimal places but for media services it may be rounded off, e.g. to 19.9 or 20 per cent.

When the currency is in a bigger denomination than the U.S. dollar and is therefore expressed as so many dollars to the currency, take the difference between the old and new rate, divide by the old rate, and multiply by 100, e.g.:

In 1967 sterling was devalued from $2.80 to $2.40. The difference, $0.40, divided by the old rate, $2.80, gives a devaluation of 14.28 per cent.

This is the method of calculation used by the International Monetary Fund and gives the international value of the currency or the change in value for a foreigner who wishes to buy the currency.

Some governments make announcements about the percentage change from a domestic standpoint – what it would cost one of their nationals to buy U.S. dollars. This can lead to confusion. Journalists should always do their own calculation on the old and new rates given.

The announcement of a realignment of currencies sometimes gives the movement against an index or basket of currencies. If this is all that is immediately available, you should find out the next exchange rate against the U.S. dollar, some other leading world currency, the International Monetary Fund's Special Drawing Right or another relevant unit of account.

In a developing currency story bear in mind the new reader, who has not been following the financial crisis, and explain the impact on the man in the street of the development you are reporting.

IMF Special Drawing Rights (SDRs) may be abbreviated at second reference. When referring to a currency spell it out, e.g. *the Canadian dollar firmed . . .* or *Sterling advanced. . . .* Do not use *Dmk*, *Sfr*, *Dkr*, etc., when referring to sums in marks, Swiss francs, Danish crowns, etc.

Use Danish/Norwegian/Swedish crowns rather than kroner, especially as the plurals are spelled differently in various Nordic languages.

currency conversions   See **conversions.**

currently   Unless you are comparing the present with the past the word is usually redundant, as in *The country currently has four million men in its armed forces.*

curtainraiser   A story filed just before an event to outline the main developments expected, with details of the venue, time of main events, security arrangements and so on. Like the advancer (**q.v.**) it should avoid a programmatic approach and emphasise issues and personalities.

cutback   Use *cut.*

cyclone   *See* **storms.**

Czech   A native of Bohemia. Do not use when you mean an *inhabitant of Czechoslovakia*, who is a *Czechoslovak.*

D

Dahomey Now *Benin*, West Africa.

Daimler-Benz Note hyphen.

Dalai Lama Tibet's most revered spiritual leader, who fled his homeland to India in 1959 after a failed uprising against Chinese rule. Born in 1935, he is seen by Tibetans as the 14th reincarnation of a long line of Buddhist god-kings. Based in northern India, the Dalai Lama heads a government-in-exile which is not recognised by any country. He was awarded the Nobel Peace Prize in 1989, much to the anger of the Chinese government. In 1988 the Dalai Lama effectively tempered his calls for Tibetan independence by proposing a five-point plan for genuine autonomy which would let China control Tibet's foreign affairs.

The Panchen Lama is the second highest figure in Tibet's spiritual hierarchy. Historically he has been closer to Beijing than has the Dalai Lama. The last Panchen Lama died during a visit to Tibet in 1989 at the age of 51. The search for his reincarnation continues.

See also **Tibet**.

dangling participle The dangling or unattached participle, in which the phrase is not properly linked to its subject, is a frequent trap for the unwary. There are cases in which it is acceptable, e.g. *Considering the risks involved, you were right to cancel the trip.* Although it is not you who is considering the risks but the writer of the sentence, the sense is clear. But avoid the dangling participle when it makes the sentence absurd, e.g. *Having disarmed, Ruritania's allies guaranteed its defence.* Here the participle *having disarmed* is wrongly attached to the allies when in fact it is Ruritania that has disarmed.

Fetching anything between 16,000 and 40,000 dollars, only some 2,500 women around the world can afford to buy haute couture dresses. The juxtaposition of *fetching* and *women* suggests it is the women not the dresses who are worth 16,000 dollars.

dashes See **punctuation.**

data Strictly a plural noun, but treat as if it were singular, e.g. *The data was corrupted.*

database Loosely used to mean any body of data held in a computer, but more precisely one in which each data item is stored only once and is related to others in a structure accessible to each user or application that might need it. In a distributed database data is held in two or more locations, possibly remote from one another, but whose physical location is transparent to the user.

dateline cities The datelines in all foreign stories should include the name of the country in the case of any city whose location cannot be assumed to be widely known outside the region where it is located.

This is particularly the case when you are writing a story from a dateline in one country about events in another country.

If the dateline of a story does not specify the country concerned then this should be made clear in the lead paragraph.

datelines News agency stories normally carry the dateline of the city from which they were filed.

Statements telephoned, faxed or telexed to news agency bureaux from people who do not work for them should, if authenticated, carry the dateline of the centre where they were received.

dates House styles vary but the sequence month/day/year seems logical, e.g. *Iraq's invasion of Kuwait on August 2, 1990* since in a shorter form you would naturally write *the August 2 invasion* rather than *the 2 August invasion.*

Do not abbreviate months in text. Write *arrived on Monday* not *arrived Monday.* Write *the 1939–45 war* but *from 1939 to 1945* not *from 1939–45.* Similarly *between 1939 and 1945* not *between 1939–45.*

daylead A news agency term for the first story issued on any topic of substance in a news cycle. Dayleads are of three main types:

1. The curtainraiser. This sets the scene for an event taking place later that day. While giving the essential facts on when and where the event is taking place and who is taking part, the curtainraiser should be more than merely programmatic. It must make clear, preferably in the lead, the significance of the event and set it in context.

2. The lead to a running story. If a story has been developing in

the six to eight hours before the daylead is written, the daylead serves the same purpose as any other lead – summarising the latest developments and putting them in context, with the strongest (which is not necessarily the latest) news point in the lead. The daylead should if possible indicate what developments are expected.

3. The recapitulation. If there have been no significant developments in the serial story in the previous six to eight hours the daylead must take a radically different approach. There is no point in simply rehashing the previous day's events, which will have been covered in late-night radio or television bulletins and in the morning papers. Go instead for a throwforward angle, predicting the next likely development, or go for a soft lead, perhaps seizing on a subsidiary angle not previously developed and exploiting that.

Whatever form of daylead you are writing, seek a fresh approach, look forward rather than backward, avoid the programmatic approach, e.g. *NATO defence ministers were on Thursday heading into their third day of talks. . . .* Even worse are tired cliches such as *President George Bush prepared on Sunday to leave for Helsinki . . ., French troops braced on Tuesday for. . . ., Kigali was calm but tense as . . . .* Dayleads tend to have a fairly short shelf life, so you can afford to experiment with technique.

If turning over old news in a daylead try to keep the time element out of the lead paragraph and use the perfect tense, not the past historic, e.g. *Chancellor Helmut Kohl has promised Germany will . . .* rather than: *Kohl promised on Tuesday Germany would. . . .*

DEA Drug Enforcement Administration (U.S.).

deaf Describe people as *deaf* only if they are totally without hearing. Otherwise write that their *hearing is impaired* or that they have *only partial hearing*.

decimals See **figures, fractions**.

decimate Literally *to reduce by one-tenth*, loosely *to reduce very heavily*. Not, however, *to virtually wipe out*.

defamation See **libel**.

default See **loans**.

defuse, diffuse To *defuse* is to make something harmless, to *diffuse* is to disperse.

delapidated   Correct spelling is *dilapidated.*

deletion   Deletion, or ellipsis, is the one way in which you may justifiably tamper with a quotation. Depending on house style, the omission of words from a quoted passage is indicated by using either three or four full stops with no space before or after, e.g. *"We will fight . . . and we will win."* If the words omitted come at the end of a sentence and are followed by another sentence in quotation marks, the third full stop is followed by a space, e.g. *"We will fight and we will win. . . . We will never surrender."* The word after the dots is capitalised if it is part of a new sentence.

   Drop words in this way only if the deletion does not alter the sense of the quote.

   Use ellipsis at the end of a sentence for dramatic effect very sparingly, e.g. *And then the Voice of Free Czechoslovakia fell silent. . . .*

denials   A denial is a denial is a denial. Do not qualify a denial, e.g. *flatly denied, categorically denied,* unless quoting someone. A no comment is not a denial. Write *declined to comment* rather than *refused to comment,* which suggests that the person you spoke to was under an obligation to comment.

depths   Convert metres to feet not yards.

despatch   Use *dispatch* for noun and verb (although *send* is better for the verb).

detente   The easing or end of strained relations between countries.

deutschemark   Not *deutschmark* for the German unit of currency. For most purposes *mark* is enough.

devaluation   See **currency**.

diaries   Diaries are essential news planning tools for all media organisations. Reporters and correspondents should be meticulous about sending to their news editors diary entries that are both timely and informative.

   A diary entry on an international event should ideally indicate the significance of the event, where, for how long and at what level a meeting is being held, whether internationally known figures are taking part, what the key points on the agenda are.

dive   *dived*, not *dove*.

dictator   Use of the word *dictator*, like that of *terrorist*, implies a value judgment, so be careful about using it unless quoting someone.

different   Use *different from* not *different to* or *than*.

diffuse, defuse   To *diffuse* is to disperse, to *defuse* is to make something harmless.

dilemma   Do not use simply to mean a problem. A dilemma is a situation in which you are faced with two (or more) undesirable alternatives.

disabled people   As with a person's sex, mention physical disabilities only if they are relevant to the story. Report disabilities without straying into sentimentality or condescension.

disassociate   *dissociate* is shorter, better.

disc, disk   Use *disk* when writing about computers, *disc* in all other contexts.

discount rate   Used notably in the United States, Germany and Japan. In the U.K. it is known as the minimum lending rate (MLR). It is the interest rate at which a central bank will discount government paper or lend money against government paper collateral.
   See also **bank rate**.

discover   *find* is shorter, better.

discreet, discrete   *discreet* is prudent while *discrete* is separate.

disinterested, uninterested   *disinterested* means impartial while *uninterested* means the opposite of interested. You can be both interested in an issue and disinterested.

disk   See **disc.**

disorientate   Use *disorient.*

dispatch   Not *despatch.* In most cases *send* is better, as of troops, aid, etc.

dispel   *dispelled.*

distances   There is a useful list of distances in statute miles between the world's leading cities in Part 2 of the *ABC World Airways Guide.*

doctor   Abbreviate to *Dr* without a full stop. House styles vary on whether to use this honorific for people whose doctorates are not in medicine but it can be used for archbishops and the like in preference to honorifics like *the Very Rev.* or *the Most Rev.*

donate   Plain *give* is simpler.

DOD   Department of Defence, the Pentagon (U.S.).

downlink   The satellite-to-earth element of a satellite link.

downplay   Write *play down.* See **cablese.**

Down's syndrome   A form of mental retardation caused by the improper splitting of chromosomes during gestation. Do not use *mongol* or *mongoloid* to refer to sufferers from this syndrome, although in subsequent references it is acceptable to refer to the adjective being commonly used because of the eye-shape, which is a noticeable symptom.

downtown   Americanism. Write *central Paris* not *downtown Paris.*

draft, draught   Use *draft* for a sketch, a detachment of men, a money order, *draught* for a drink or the depth to which a ship sinks in water.

dramatic   A much overworked word. If an event is dramatic this should be clear from the story.

draught   See *draft.*

drugs   The most widely used narcotic drugs are:
   Cocaine: Derived from the leaf of the coca bush, grown primarily in Peru,

Bolivia and Colombia. A powerful stimulant, cocaine is sold as a white powder which is usually "snorted" (inhaled through the nose). Dissolved, it can be injected. Street names: *coke, snow, Lady C.*

Crack: A smokeable form of cocaine made by mixing cocaine powder with water, baking soda or ammonia. The mixture is boiled into "rocks" of off-white colour. The name crack is said to stem from the crackling sound produced when the crystals are smoked.

Heroin: Derived from the opium poppy. A narcotic, heroin can be smoked, snorted or injected. Main producing areas are Southeast Asia (the "Golden Triangle" of Burma, Laos and Thailand), Southwest Asia (Afghanistan, Pakistan, Iran) and Mexico. Comes in various forms, depending on how it is administered, from powder to a gum-like substance. Street names: *H, horse, smack.*

Hashish: The resinous sap of the cannabis plant which is dried and pressed into bricks or cakes. Good quality hashish has the consistency of putty. Pieces are broken off and smoked, either in hashish pipes (the preferred form in the Middle East and Asia) or in cigarettes mixed with tobacco.

Hashish oil: Produced through repeated extraction of cannabis resin in a process similar to percolating coffee. It yields a dark, viscous liquid which is usually dripped on to cigarettes. Popular in Canada.

Marijuana: Derived from the cannabis plant. A hallucinogen, marijuana is the tobacco-like substance produced from the leaves and flowering tops of the plant. These are usually rolled into cigarettes ("joints") and smoked. The most potent marijuana is sinsemilla (Spanish for seedless) which is made from the unpollinated female cannabis plant. Biggest sinsemilla producer: the United States, where marijuana is the most widely used illegal drug. Street names: *grass, weed.* Regional labels for marijuana include *bhang* (West Africa) and *ganja* (Jamaica).

Druze   Not *Druse.* A secretive breakaway sect of Islam whose adherents live mainly in the mountains of Lebanon, Syria and Israel.

DTP   Desk-top publishing.

Duesseldorf   Not *Dusseldorf*, Germany.

duplex   Describes a circuit that can handle simultaneous two-way traffic. Half-duplex circuits can handle only one direction at a time. Full duplex is more effective for error correction.

dyke   Use *dike.*

dynamo   *dynamos.*

E

earthquakes There are several scales for measuring earthquakes, the most widely used being the American-devised Richter scale and the 12-point international Mercalli scale. Richter measures a quake's general magnitude; Mercalli describes its intensity as shown by its effect at a particular place.

If you have a choice of scale in reporting an earthquake, use Richter.

Richter:

The Richter scale does not assess effects. It gives the strength of an earthquake in terms of the energy released, as measured by seismographs. The scale starts at 1 and has no upper limit. It is logarithmic: each unit is 10 times greater than the one before.

As the Richter scale means little to the average person, you should explain it in terms of the potential effect. Refer to the known effects of a previous earthquake of similar magnitude or compare the Richter reading with that of the last major earthquake.

Earthquakes below 4 on the Richter scale are unlikely to produce major stories. Force 4 and 5 are often described as "powerful enough to cause heavy damage in a populated area".

Force 6 can cause widespread damage, while around force 8 the comparisons are with the quakes in San Francisco (1906, since calculated as 8.3 Richter) and Mexico (1985, 8.1).

There have been no recordings of a force 9 earthquake. Theoretically, there is no limit but it is not helpful to speak of the scale as "open-ended".

The most devastating earthquake in recorded history hit China's Shaanxi province in 1556, killing 830,000 people.

China suffered the worst quake in its modern history on July 28, 1976. At least 240,000 people were killed when the northeastern city of Tangshan was almost completely levelled. The Richter reading was 7.8.

Mercalli:

After experts have visited the scene of an earthquake, it may be assigned a degree on the 12-point Mercalli scale.

If the Mercalli scale is used the story should make clear that it measures not the general magnitude but the quake's intensity as shown by its effect at a particular site.

An earthquake of force 4 on the Richter scale could be listed as degree 8 on the Mercalli scale at a place near the epicentre and as degree 2 further away.

The first four Mercalli degrees are very minor; then:

5. Furniture shakes and church bells may ring, but there is little or no damage.

6. Plaster falls, lights swing, sleepers are wakened, trees shake, bells ring and there is some general alarm.

7. Windows break, defective chimneys fall and cracks appear in walls, but well-made buildings and flexible tropical houses remain intact.

8. Cracks appear in even well-built houses, and many chimneys, statues and church towers are toppled, possibly causing serious damage.

9. Houses are seriously damaged and a few buildings destroyed.

10. Most stone buildings are razed, bridges and solid wooden buildings are damaged or destroyed, water and gas main pipes are ruptured, crevasses appear in the earth and in streets.

11. All stone buildings and even the best-built bridges are destroyed, railway lines are twisted, dikes broken, and only a few flexible wooden structures survive.

12. Nothing is left of anything man-made, and the topography is changed e.g. by the formation of new lakes, huge falls of rock and major earth faults.

East   Capitalise it when used in a political sense.

East Europe   Capitalise both words.

East Germany   Write *East Germany* when referring to the former Communist state but *east Germany* when referring to the eastern part of unified Germany.

EC   European Community. Its 12 members in 1992: Belgium, Britain, Denmark, France, Germany, Greece, Ireland, Italy, Luxembourg, the Netherlands, Portugal and Spain. At second reference simply *the Community*. You can use *EC* as an adjective at first reference as long as it is clear from the context what is meant.

The European Commission may be described at second reference as *the Commission* (upper case) or *the EC executive*. It is responsible for proposing EC legislation and implementing EC law.

In the 1986 Single European Act the European Community set itself the goal of abolishing all barriers to the free movement of goods, services, capital and people by the end of 1992. A vast programme of legislation was drawn up to inject cross-border competition into protected industries, harmonise basic industrial standards and agree on common minimum rules where necessary. The "1992" programme captured the imagination of business and many ordinary citizens. Coinciding with (and at times fuelling) the economic boom of the late 1980s, it helped make the European Community the focal point of political and economic activity and the dominant force on the continent after the fall of the Iron Curtain. That in turn produced pressure for negotiations on economic and monetary union and deeper political union within the EC.

Central and East European countries have rushed to forge closer links with the Community since the collapse of communism. The Community, which already had limited trade and cooperation agreements with some states, offered financial assistance in co-ordination with other leading industrialised states on condition that countries implement democratic and market reforms. In addition, new association agreements were negotiated with Poland, Hungary and Czechoslovakia providing for extra trade concessions, more financial aid, enhanced cooperation and a regular political dialogue. The "Europe" accords also foresee the possibility of eventual membership of the Community, the declared goal of all three countries. But they are not expected to be economically strong enough for membership at least until the end of the century. Exploratory talks for negotiating similar agreements have begun with Bulgaria and Romania.

ECA Economic Commision for Africa (U.N. – Addis Ababa).

ECE Economic Commission for Europe (U.N. – Geneva).

ECLAC Economic Commission for Latin America and the Caribbean (U.N. – Santiago, Chile).

economic, economical *economic* has to do with economics, *economical* means thrifty.

economic indicators The major economic indicators are consumer or producer price indices, wholesale prices, industrial production, unemployment, money supply, trade and balance of payments data, reserves and GNP/GDP.

Where appropriate, all indicators should contain the current month's figure or percentage, the previous month's figure or percentage and the figure for the month one year earlier. The base year for the index and the index for the current month should be included where available. Other index comparisons are not necessary.

If the figures are provisional, say so. Say also if they are unadjusted or adjusted. Use the adjusted data if it is available. Annual rate figures have no adjustment factor since the seasonal influence is no longer relevant.

If a figure is revised upwards or downwards give the comparison with the first provisional estimate.

ECSC European Coal and Steel Community (Luxembourg). It has the same 12 members as the European Community.

Ecu The European currency unit, a notional EC currency based on a basket of its 12 member-currencies with each country's share weighted according to its share of EC output. The value of the Ecu against the U.S. dollar is not fixed, so do not convert Ecu figures in media stories into dollars at par. Give the Ecu figure, followed by the dollar figure in brackets.

When the rate is at par do not bracket the same figures, only the currency name. Examples: *250,000 Ecus (265,000 dollars)* but *26 million Ecus (dollars)*.

See also **currency**.

Ecuadorean Not *Ecuadoran*.

effect See **affect**.

EFTA European Free Trade Association. Its seven members in 1992: Austria, Finland, Iceland, Liechtenstein, Norway, Sweden and Switzerland.

Eid al-Adha A Moslem holiday marking the climax of the annual pilgrimage (haj) on the 10th day of the 12th month of the Moslem calendar.

Eid al-Fitr A Moslem holiday marking the end of the fasting month of Ramadan, the ninth month of the Moslem calendar.

Eire Use *Republic of Ireland*.

either . . . or The verb that follows should agree in number with the subject nearer to it, e.g. *Either Thailand or Malaysia and Singapore are likely to be the next in line* not *Either Thailand or Malaysia and Singapore is likely to be the next in line*.

El Al *El Al Israeli Airlines* is the full name but *El Al* is acceptable as long as the second reference makes clear it is the Israeli company.

electronic news gathering Video recording of television news coverage, as opposed to filming.

electronic mail A computerised messaging system in which messages are held centrally but can be read only by addressees.

elevation Height, or angle in the vertical plane, e.g. for pointing a dish at a satellite.

ellipsis Use ellipsis at the end of a sentence for dramatic effect very sparingly, e.g. *And then the Voice of Free Czechoslovakia fell silent. . . .* For ellipses in a quotation see **deletions**.

embarass Correct spelling is *embarrass*.

embargo A legal ban on trade. A boycott is the refusal of a group to deal with a person or use a commodity.

embargoes News agencies use two kinds of embargo, a transmission embargo and a publication embargo. In a transmission embargo the source of the information provides it to the agency on the understanding that no story will be transmitted until a specified time. A publication embargo permits immediate transmission of a story but with an advisory line telling users that it may not be published or broadcast before a certain time.

If you obtain from an independent source news that is the subject of material already received under embargo, you may legitimately issue your own unembargoed story. Your knowledge of an embargo should not inhibit any attempts previously set in train to pursue a story.

embarrass   Two *rs*. Not *embarass*.

emotive words   Some words have emotional significance and should be used with special care in the interest of objectivity. Most media organisations have a clear policy on this issue. But in general you should bear in mind that the unqualified use of words like *terrorist, terrorism, extremist* or *extremism* can be read as meaning that you consider them to be objectively accurate labels. Use of the word *insurgent* should also be discriminating.

One man's terrorist is another man's freedom-fighter. One man's insurgent may be another man's lawful ruler driving out usurpers.

Avoid using contentious labels as far as possible. If you must use one like *a terrorist act* you should be conscious that by doing so you and your newspaper are implicitly judging the action as a breach of normal moral standards and taking sides.

You can, of course, use such words without inhibition when directly quoting sources that are named or individually identified.

There are alternatives to *terrorist* that are more objectively factual, e.g. *gunmen, bombers, bomb attacks, assassinations*.

The word *guerrillas* can be more readily used when describing such large forces as the Afghan rebels or left-wing forces fighting right-wing governments in Central America.

Relatively small groups are usually best described by their ideologies or politics – anarchist, nationalist, right-wing, left-wing, etc.

Also see **background, cliches, mob, neutral verbs, terrorism**.

EMS   The European Monetary System of the European Community. Created in 1979, it includes all 12 EC countries. Their currencies determine the value of the EC's composite currency, the European currency unit (Ecu) (**q.v.**). With Portugal's entry in April 1992, 11 EC countries take part in the system's Exchange Rate Mechanism

(ERM). The exception is Greece which must join by January 1, 1994. The ERM limits to 2.25% the maximum fluctuation of member currencies against each other but three of the 11 currencies – the pound sterling, peseta and escudo – are temporarily allowed to move up or down by a maximum of 6%.

England   Do not use *England* when you mean *Britain* or *the United Kingdom* or *English* when you mean *British*. See **Britain**.

en route   Not *on route.*

enquire, enquiry   Use *inquire, inquiry.*

enrol   *enrolled, enrolment.*

ensure, insure   *ensure* means to make sure, *insure* to guarantee against loss.

envision   Use *envisage.*

EPA   Environmental Protection Agency (U.S.).

EPS   Earnings per share. A means of gauging how much return a company gives on its ordinary share capital. It is calculated by dividing the net income of the company by the number of shares in issue.

ERM   The Exchange Rate Mechanism (of the European Monetary System. See **EMS**.)

escalate, escalation   Fancy words beloved of journalists who think that long words give their copy an air of authority or profound thought. In most cases *rise* or *increase* would be simpler and as effective for both verb and noun. *Escalate* may usefully be used when referring to a step-by-step increase.

ESCAP   Economic and Social Commission for Asia and the Pacific (U.N. – Bangkok).

ESCWA   Economic and Social Commission for Western Asia (U.N. – Amman).

Esfahan   Not *Isfahan*, Iran.

etcetera   Use the abbreviation *etc.* (with full stop).

Ethiopian names   The word *ato* means *Mr.* Use only the first name at second reference, e.g. *Mengistu Haile Mariam – Mengistu said. . . .*

euphemism Euphemism, beloved of bureaucrats and social scientists, seeks to cloak reality, sometimes unpleasant, in innocuous words. Shun it. Except in quotation, write *cheap* not *low-cost*, *elderly people* not *senior citizens*, *poor* not *disadvantaged*.

Euratom European Atomic Energy Community (Brussels), composed of the 12 European Community members.

Euromarkets An overall term for international capital markets dealing in Eurobonds, Eurocredits, etc. Use it only in general stories about Euromarkets as a whole; otherwise specify which market is meant, e.g. *Prices fall sharply on Eurobond market* not *Prices fall sharply on Euromarkets*. See also **bonds, loans**.

European If the context of a story is racial it is better to use *white* than *European*.

European names Use lower case for particles within a personal name, e.g. *F. W. de Klerk, Maurice de la Haye, Richard von Weizsaecker, Miguel de la Madrid, Ramon da Silva, Jaime Aragon y Galicia, Hendrik van den Berg*. The particles are usually retained at second reference, but in German usage the *von* is dropped.

Upper case is used when such particles occur at the beginning of a geographical name, e.g. *Las Palmas, El Salvador, La Raya del Palancar* or at the start of a sentence, e.g. *De Klerk said. . . .*

See also **Hispanic names**.

Eutelsat European Telecommunications Satellite Organisation, set up by 26 European governments to run an international satellite system.

evoke, invoke *evoke* means to bring to mind, *invoke* to call upon solemnly, e.g. *In a speech evoking memories of the civil war he invoked God's help in preventing fresh bloodshed*.

ex- In using this prefix make sure it is hyphenated to the word it limits. Note the difference between *a Conservative ex-minister* and *an ex-Conservative minister*.

While *ex-* may be used for brevity in headlines, e.g. *EX-MINISTER KILLED IN BRAZIL AIR CRASH*, prefer *former* in text, e.g. *Former Brazilian finance minister Jorge Braga was killed on Tuesday when. . . .*

exchange rates   House styles vary but in general you normally quote only a single rate for the value of one currency against another. This is the middle rate between the bid and offer quotations.

For example, if the bid and offer rates of a particular currency against the dollar were 2.6050 and 2.6150 you would take the difference between the two (0.0100), halve it (0.0050) and add to 2.6050. This gives a rate of 2.61. If the difference is an odd number, quote as near to the mid-point as possible.

In specialist business stories rate can be reported as a traded price, i.e. 1.9408 dlrs to the pound or as a quote – the buy (bid) and sell (offer) rates together, separated in most cases by a slash /, e.g. 1.6770/80.

Most markets give quotes in that order, so that the lower bid rate comes first, but local practice can vary, as in the U.K. money market. Do not estimate the traded level by giving the midprice of the bid and offered rates.

Do not repeat recurring numbers when giving the second rate in the sequence, e.g. 1.4845/65 not 1.4845/4865.

So a currency rate would be written: *The dollar rose to 1.4895/ 1.4905 marks from 1.4850/60 at yesterday's close.* Note that currencies are always quoted as rising or falling TO the new figure FROM the former one, not from/to.

Currency rates are generally carried to four places right of the decimal, except for yen, which goes to two places. However, if both bid and offer are round numbers at fewer decimal places, leave off the extra zeros.

Money market rates and bond prices are generally quoted in fractions up to 16ths and 32nds, so it looks cleaner to quote the traded price, e.g. 99-1/4, than to link many numbers and slashes by quoting the bid and offered levels. Prices should be given in the lowest denominator, e.g. 99-1/4 not 99-8/32.

If the bid/offer quote were important you could say 99-1/4 1/2, separating the two with a space. Quotes on either side of the "big figure" should be separated with commas, e.g. 99-3/4, 100-1/4.

Note that many issues in the bond or money markets are so large that the bid and offered spreads are narrower than fractions and are normally quoted in decimal form, e.g. 101.25/27.

For bond futures prices are often written in 32nds. For other futures they are written in basis points (one one-hundredth of a point). Note one exception – German government bond (bund) futures are also written in basis points. Thus the long gilt contract trades at 89-10/32, the bund at 83.23 and the short sterling contract at 86.73.

To give the bond or bond futures quote in 32nds, write 89-10/32 18/32 and separate quotes on either side of the "big figure" with commas, e.g. 89-31/32, 90-7/32. The decimal quote for futures would be 83.23/25.

expatriate Not *expatriot* or *ex-patriot*.

expect, anticipate These are not synonyms. If you anticipate something you not only expect it but also take precautionary action to deal with it.

extremist See **emotive words**.

eyeing Not *eying*.

F

FAA   Federal Aviation Administration (U.S.).

facility   A word that can mean almost anything. Be specific if possible, e.g. *a base, a factory, a depot*.

facility fees   See **loans**.

Fahrenheit   See **temperatures**.

Falklands   This is the internationally accepted name of the Falkland Islands but from an Argentine dateline they may also be called by the Argentine name – *the Malvinas (Falkland Islands)*.

Fannie Mae   Federal National Mortgage Association (FNMA), a U.S. government-sponsored corporation owned entirely by private stockholders. It buys and sells residential mortgages. See also **Ginnie Mae**.

FAO   Food and Agriculture Organisation (U.N. – Rome).

Faroes   Not *Faeroes*.

farther, farthest   Use *further/furthest* except when referring to physical distance.

FBI   Federal Bureau of Investigation (U.S.). So well known that the initials may be used alone at first reference. If the full name is used alone at first reference the initials need not be bracketed in.

FCC   Federal Communications Commission (U.S.).

FDA   Food and Drug Administration (U.S.).

FDM   Frequency division multiplexing. See **multiplexer**.

FDP   Free Democratic party (Germany).

fears, hopes   Beware of hopes and fears. Unattributed, they represent opinions. You should not refer to hopes for a settlement of Middle East problems or fears of another oil price increase without saying who is doing the hoping or fearing. But you can refer unsourced to the common hopes and fears of humanity, e.g. *Hopes of reaching the trapped miners rose. . . .* or *Fears that a new epidemic of cholera might sweep . . . .*

See also **emotive words**.

features   Features provide an opportunity to analyse both specific events and trends in a depth and with a quality of writing that it is not always possible to bring to a spot story under the pressure of deadlines. They are also a medium in which to report human interest, arts, entertainment, scientific, medical and environmental stories that do not have a specific spot angle.

Newspapers are more likely to use a feature if there is a news picture or news graphic to go with it.

fedayeen   Arab or Islamic guerrillas. The singular is *feda'i* so use *guerrilla* for simplicity's sake when referring to one person.

fellah   Egyptian peasant. Plural *fellahin*.

FEP   A computer's front end processor.

fewer, less than   Use *fewer* when referring to numbers of individuals or individual items, *less* for quantities, e.g. *Fewer than 10 rescuers were hurt* but *Less than 1,000 tons of coal was lost.*

fiance, fiancee   *fiance* is the man, *fiancee* the woman.

fiasco   *fiascos*.

field   An element of data with a set number of characters, typically appearing in a fixed position in a screen display, such as a story header.

field marshal   Note only one *l* in *marshal*.

FIFA   International Football Federation (soccer – Zurich).

fighter jets   Write *jet fighters* (if indeed you need the word jet at all, since modern fighters are almost invariably jets).

figures   House styles vary but usually the digits one to nine are spelled out in text except for dates and times, when figures should always be used, e.g. *The four foreign ministers will meet at 6 p.m. (1700 GMT) on March 3.*

Write 10 and above as figures except at the start of a sentence, e.g. *Fourteen people were killed when 20 tons of ice crashed through the roof.* Do not however start a sentence with a complex figure, e.g. *Two hundred and forty-three runners finished the Boston marathon. . . .* Note that some editors would spell out the words one to ten, not one to nine.

Do not run two sets of figures together. This can lead to errors. Separate them by a word or spell out one of the two, e.g. *20,000 ten-pound notes* not *20,000 10-pound notes.*

Round off unwieldy figures, e.g. *Japan produced 1.45 million cars in the six months ended. . . .* not *Japan produced 1,453,123 cars. . . .* As a rule round off millions to the nearest 10,000, thousands to the nearest 100, hundreds to the nearest 10.

Where totals do not add up because of rounding, this should be explained. If a company announces a dividend of, say, 0.123456 pence per share, do not round it off.

Figures are normally rounded to two significant decimals, with halves rounded upwards. Thus *15.564* becomes *15.56,* while *15.565* becomes *15.57.*

If a country adjusts its currency, any rate given must not be rounded off, e.g. *France announced a rate of 5.79831 francs to the Ecu.*

When reporting decimalised figures Anglo-Saxon publications use a full stop, e.g. *42.5* while continental Europe uses a comma instead of a decimal point.

It is better to spell out *billion.*

filibuster   Not *fillibuster.* To delay parliamentary proceedings by making long speeches.

Filipino   A native of the Philippines. Feminine *Filipina.* Plural *Filipinos.* The adjective is *Philippine.*

film titles   House styles vary but normally a title is either put in italics or in quotation marks. Capitalise every word in the title apart from conjunctions, articles, particles, and short prepositions, e.g. *"A Night at the Opera".*

finalise   *complete* or *finish* is better.

first, second, third   Use these words rather than *firstly, secondly, thirdly,* etc.

first lady   Do not capitalise. Avoid such arch terms as *first dog,* unless in direct quotations.

First World War   Or *World War One.* Not *WWI.*

flabby phrases *Come, leave* and *give* are verbs too often misused in phrases such as: *The demands came when . . ., The fire left six people dead, The strike left housewives angry* or *The move gave a boost to . . . .*

Demands don't come; people make them. Fires kill people, rather than leave them dead. Strikes anger housewives. Moves boost things.

This came as that happened is a construction that too frequently infects journalists' copy, often at the expense of brevity and sense, e.g. *Major's speech came as U.S. Secretary of State James Baker landed at Heathrow.* Ten to one Major was not speaking as Baker's plane landed; and even if he did why not simply *Major spoke as . . .?*

Avoid also *continued* and *reiterated* which give the impression of monotonous action and are unlikely to attract the reader.

See also **cliches, jargon**.

flack, flak *flack* is an American slang term for a public relations man, to be used only if explained. *flak* is anti-aircraft fire or heavy criticism.

flair, flare A *flair* is a talent. A *flare* is an illuminating device.

flash The term used by some news agencies to indicate their top-priority stories. A flash normally consists of only a few words but should have a brief source. See also **bulletin, urgent**.

flaunt, flout To *flaunt* is to display ostentatiously (not just to display), to *flout* is to defy, e.g. *By flaunting your wealth you flout convention.*

flight numbers When scheduled flights come into the news – crashes, hijackings, bomb scares, etc. – give the flight number together with other identification such as type of aircraft, airline, destination and route.

flout See **flaunt**.

flyer Not *flier*.

focus focused.

follow-up Once you start reporting a story you should report the sequel, if there is one. This applies particularly to court cases where you may have reported allegations against individuals or groups of people that may not be upheld by the verdict.

If one company announces that it is planning to bid for another, the second company should be contacted for reaction.

following   Prefer *after* as a preposition, e.g. *After the crash* . . . not *Following the crash* . . . .

foodstuffs, food supplies   In most cases *food* is enough.

foot   To convert roughly to metres multiply by 3 and divide by 10; to convert precisely multiply by 0.305.

footprint   The area of the globe covered by a particular satellite's signal. Also, the area of a desk covered by a PC or other device.

forbear, forebear   *forbear* means to refrain, a *forebear* is an ancestor.

forego, forgo   *forego* is to precede; *forgo* to do without.

foreign language words and phrases   Use these only in exceptional cases, for instance where no generally recognised equivalent exists in your own language. In English prefer *blank cheque* or *free hand* to *carte blanche*, *skirmish* to *melee*, *indefinitely* to *ad infinitum* and *yearly* to *per annum*.

Always explain foreign phrases, e.g. *Dismissing the libel action, the judge said: "De minimis non curat lex" (a Latin phrase meaning "The law does not concern itself with very small matters".)*

forex   *forex* can be used as shorthand to describe the foreign exchange market but it is better to use the full description. Forex is also a club grouping foreign exchange dealers. Each major foreign exchange dealing centre has its own forex club.

format   *formatted.*

formula   *formulas.*

forum   *forums.*

fractions   In everyday life people think in fractions not decimals. So in stories where mathematical precision is not essential use *a quarter, a third, a half* rather than *25, 33, 50 per cent.* In a lead on an opinion poll, for instance, it is better to write: *Two Germans in three prefer* . . . than *Sixty-nine per cent of Germans prefer.* . . . The precise figure should be given lower in the story. Hyphenate fractions like *two-thirds, three-quarters.*

front-end loading   This describes the structure of life-assurance investment policies that impose heavy penalties on investors cashing in before their fixed term has ended because the management charges are deducted at the outset.

front line   Normally two words, but hyphenated as adjective, e.g. *front-line positions.*

front-line states   The African countries confronting South Africa are Angola, Botswana, Mozambique, Namibia, Tanzania, Zambia and Zimbabwe.

FTC   Federal Trade Commission (U.S.).

fuel   *fuelled.*

fulfil   *fulfilled* but *fulfilment.*

fulsome   Not *fullsome.* It is not a synonym for lavish. *Fulsome praise* is praise that is excessive and fawning.

futures   Standardised contracts for the purchase or sale of financial instruments or physical commodities for future delivery on a commodity exchange.

G

G5   The five largest capitalist economies: the United States, Japan, Germany, France and the United Kingdom. Their governments meet informally to discuss general economic questions and specific issues like exchange rates and foreign debt. Their currencies constitute the IMF's SDR (**q.v.**).

G7   The seven largest capitalist economies, comprising G5 plus Italy and Canada. G7 heads of state or government meet annually.

G10   The 10 leading capitalist economies comprising the G7, Belgium, the Netherlands and Sweden. Now joined by Switzerland to make 11 but still referred to as the G10. It works within the framework of the IMF (**q.v.**) to create as stable a world economic system as possible by coordinating members' fiscal and monetary policies.

G24   A group of developing countries formed to represent their interests in negotiations on international monetary matters. In 1992 they were Algeria, Argentina, Brazil, Colombia, Egypt, Ethiopia, Gabon, Ghana, Guatemala, India, Iran, Ivory Coast, Lebanon, Mexico, Nigeria, Pakistan, Peru, Philippines, Sri Lanka, Syria, Trinidad and Tobago, Venezuela, Yugoslavia and Zaire.
   A separate G-24 was formed in 1990 with the same membership as the OECD industrial nations (**q.v.**) to provide financial support for reforms in East European countries. It is coordinated by the EC (**q.v.**) and meets in Brussels.

G77   Originally established with 77 but now comprising 127 countries. Set up to help promote the views of developing countries on international trade and development in UNCTAD (**q.v.**).

Gaborone   Not *Gabarone*, Botswana.

gales   Better than *gale-force winds*. A gale is less powerful than a storm (**q.v.**) in nautical parlance.

gallon   To convert Imperial gallons roughly to litres multiply by 9 and divide by 2, precisely multiply by 4.546.

To convert U.S. gallons roughly to litres multiply by 4, precisely multiply by 3.785.

To convert Imperial gallons roughly to U.S. gallons multiply by 6 and divide by 5, precisely multiply by 1.201.

To convert U.S. gallons roughly to Imperial gallons multiply by 5 and divide by 6, precisely multiply by 0.833.

See **measures**.

Gambia   Not *the Gambia*, West Africa.

gambit   Not simply an opening move (in chess or metaphorically) but one that involves a sacrifice. *Opening gambit* is tautological.

Gandhi   Not *Ghandi*.

ganja   See **drugs – marijuana**.

gaol   Use *jail*.

gas   *gases*. Use *petrol* rather than *gas* when referring to the fuel.

GATT   General Agreement on Tariffs and Trade (U.N. – Geneva). The initials may be used by themselves at first reference with the full name given lower in the story. Do no write *the GATT*.

gay   As the word is now universally used as a synonym for homosexual (**q.v.**), it is better not to use it in other senses.

GCC   Gulf Cooperation Council (Riyadh). Its six members are Bahrain, Kuwait, Oman, Qatar, Saudi Arabia and the United Arab Emirates.

GDP   The gross domestic product is similar to GNP (**q.v.**) but omits income from abroad.

gearing   The amount of debt a company has in proportion to its total assets.

gender   See *sexist language*.

general   Hyphenate *brigadier-general, lieutenant-general, major-general*. At second reference just *the general*. In the U.S. army a brigadier-general has one star, a major-general two, a lieutenant-general three and a general four. The British army has the rank of brigadier but not of brigadier-general.

Gentile   Anyone not a Jew. Capitalise.

geographical and geological names   Capitalise these, apart from particles, articles, and compass references not forming part of the proper name, e.g. *the River Plate* but *the river*; *North Korea* but *north London*; *the Nile Delta* but *the delta of the Nile*; *the Upper Pleistocene*; *the lower East Side of New York* but *the lower east bank of the river*.

Germany   The united Germany, like the former West Germany, is formally called the Federal Republic of Germany. Berlin is capital of the united Germany but Bonn is the seat of government. Write *East Germany* when referring to the former Communist state but *east* or *west Germany* when referring to the eastern and western parts of the unified Germany.

ghetto   *ghettos*.

GI   A U.S. soldier (from *government issue*). Use only in informal contexts.

giant   Do not use when describing companies. In general avoid this cliche.

Gibraltar, Strait of   Not *Straits*.

GIBs   Guaranteed income bonds. Insurance-based products that will pay a fixed regular income over a fixed period, at the end of which the capital is returned to the investor.

gift   Leave *free gifts* to the advertising world. A gift is by definition free.

Ginnie Mae   Government National Mortgage Association (GNMA). Set up in the United States in 1968 to take over some of the functions of the Fannie Mae (**q.v.**). Securities issued by the GNMA are backed by pools of mortgages, bear a U.S. government guarantee and are traded in an active secondary market.

gipsy   Use *gypsy*.

girl   Do not write *girl* when you mean *woman*. As a rule of thumb, a girl becomes a woman at 18.
    See also **sexist language**.

glamorise   Not *glamourise*.

global   Beware of excessive use. *Global* is correct for the threat of global warming, i.e. something that affects the whole globe.

However companies sometimes talk of their *global network* which is an exaggeration unless they are represented in all the business centres on the globe. Use *world* instead.

GMT Greenwich Mean Time. As the international standard it is not spelled out but should be capitalised. Western military forces use Zulu to mean GMT. It is necessary to convert a local time into GMT, e.g. *8.30 a.m. (1330 GMT)*, only when the Greenwich time is relevant to the rest of the world, such as the moment that an earthquake struck.

GNP The gross national product is the total value of goods and services produced within a period of time by an economy, including government and private spending, fixed capital investment, net inventory change and net exports.

See also **GDP**.

good, bad Whether news is good or bad news may depend on who you are. A fall in the price of sugar may be good news for the Dutch housewife but bad for a Brazilian sugar-cutter. Use these phrases with care.

gourmand, gourmet A *gourmand* is a glutton, a *gourmet* an epicure.

governor-general *governors-general.* Note hyphen.

government ministers Unless your house style dictates otherwise, capitalise a ministerial title at first reference when it precedes the full name. When the title follows the name or is used alone, use lower case, e.g.: *French Foreign Minister Roland Dumas*; *Roland Dumas, the French foreign minister*; *the foreign minister*. *President George Bush* but *The president said. . . .*

governmental bodies Again subject to a contrary ruling in your house style, treat governmental and legislative bodies as proper names, capitalising them when an integral part of a specific name but not when unspecific as in plurals or standing alone, e.g. *The Israeli Foreign Ministry* or *the Foreign Ministry said Israel would. . . .* but *the ministry said*; *the Australian Parliament* but *the Australian and New Zealand parliaments*; *the EC Executive Commission* but *the commission*. An exception is *the European Community* which is *the Community* at second reference.

grace period See **loans**.

graffiti   Scribbling on a wall. This is a plural noun, the singular being *graffito*.

gram   Not *gramme*. Likewise *kilogram*. Convert to ounces for weights up to 400 grams, to pounds for larger weights.

To convert roughly to ounces divide by 30, precisely multiply by 0.035. To convert roughly to pounds multiply by 2 and divide by 900, precisely multiply by 0.0022. See also **measures**.

gray   Use *grey*.

Great Britain   England, Scotland and Wales.

grisly, grizzly   *grisly* means *frightful, hideous, horrible*. *grizzly* means *grey, greyish, grey-haired*, as in *grizzly bear*.

grovel   *grovelled*.

guerrilla   Not *guerilla*. See **emotive words, terrorism**.

Gulf   The most neutral term to use for the Middle East Gulf. Avoid either *Arabian* or *Persian Gulf* unless you want to take sides in an Arab-Iranian semantic and political dispute. Write *the Gulf of Mexico* in full at first reference.

guns   See **weapons**.

Gurkha   Not *Ghurka*.

guttural   Not *gutteral*.

gypsy   Not *gipsy*.

H

Haarlem, Harlem   *Haarlem* is in the Netherlands, *Harlem* in New York City.

habeas corpus   Not *habeus*. A writ to produce a prisoner before a court.

Habsburg   Not *Hapsburg*.

haj   Not *hadj, hajj*. A Moslem pilgrimage to Mecca.

haji   One who has performed the haj.

handgun   One word. A weapon that can be held and fired in one hand, e.g. a pistol. Rifles and shotguns are not handguns. See **weapons**.

hang   A person is *hanged*, a picture *hung*.

hangar   Not *hanger*.

Hapsburg   Use *Habsburg*.

hara-kiri   Japanese ritual suicide. Not *hari-kari*.

harass   One R. Not *harrass*.

hard copy   Copy in paper form as opposed to a story in electronic form on a VDT.

hard leads   See **soft leads**.

hashish   See **drugs**.

he/she, he or she   Avoid these clumsy usages; likewise *him/her* and *him or her*. The easiest way is to use the plural form, e.g. *Journalists should write simple English. They should . . .* not *A journalist should write simple English. He or she should. . . .*

header   At the top of a screen display, this contains all necessary information about a story or message except the text itself. It is set out in pre-assigned fields so the information can be translated for each receiving system to handle the story appropriately.

headlines   Headline writing is an art in itself, best learned by practice. It places a premium on the ability to capture the gist of a story in a few crisp words that will intrigue readers and persuade them to read the story that follows.

The constraints of space require headline writers to use the shortest words possible, and herein lie two dangers – over-reliance on cliches and the importing of headline-ese into text, where atrophied monosyllables are used instead of literate English, e.g.: *President George Bush may move to bring back the draft in a bid to boost.* . . .

hectare   To convert roughly to acres multiply by 5 and divide by 2; to convert precisely multiply by 2.471.

heights   Convert the heights of mountains, buildings, etc., to feet (not yards) from metres.

here   Avoid using *here* as a device to locate the action of a story. It can lead to confusion, ambiguity and sometimes error. It is often not necessary to give a locator in a lead paragraph. For instance, in a Budapest-datelined story on a meeting between the Hungarian and French presidents one would assume that they met in the capital unless the story explicitly said otherwise. In that case the reference to the location could come in the second or third paragraph.

heroin   See **drugs**.

HEW   Department of Health, Education and Welfare (U.S.).

hi-tech   Use as an adjective only. As a noun write *high technology*.

hike   Americanism. Use *rise* when referring to an increase in pay, prices, etc.

hippie   Not *hippy*. A rebel against middle-class values.

Hispanic names   People in Spanish-speaking countries usually include in their full names the family name of their father followed by that of their mother, sometimes linked by *y* (and), e.g. *Ferdinand Maradona Lopez, Pedro Ardiles y Portillo*.

Give the full name at first reference, but only the father's family name (*Maradona, Ardiles*) at second reference, unless the person is normally known by the combination of two names.

historic, historical   A *historic* event is a major and dramatic one, a *historical* event is one which, even if in itself quite minor, is part of history. *Historic* is nearly always the word you need. Use *historic* sparingly. Do not proclaim every second news event as historic. Most have a limited shelf life. Let history itself decide what will one day be regarded as truly historic.

Hitler First name was *Adolf* not *Adolph*. His title was *Fuehrer* (leader) not *Fuhrer*.

hoard, horde A *hoard* is a *hidden stock* or *treasure*, a *horde* a *multitude*.

hoaxes Be constantly on guard against hoax attempts. Be suspicious and check sources. Do not use news until its authenticity has been proved.

Most hoax attempts can be parried by following this drill: Regard all information you receive by telephone as suspect unless you know the caller. If you do not, ask for full name, title and telephone number. Also ask for the switchboard number to call back on to ensure that the call is coming from the company identified by the caller.

Make an independent check of the name and number, then telephone back. Get confirmation that it was indeed this person who telephoned you.

Use the same precautions with unsolicited material received by fax or telex.

Be on guard against April Fool hoaxes and all fantasies such as the birth of five-legged sheep, human pregnancies lasting 18 months, the marriage of 100-year-old sweethearts, perfect bridge hands and miracles.

Holland Use *the Netherlands*.

holocaust Wholesale slaughter or destruction by fire. Capitalise when referring to the Nazi massacre of European Jewry in 1939–45.

Holy Places The Holy Places of Islam are Mecca, Medina and Jerusalem, in that order. In Mecca it is the great mosque containing the Kaaba (**q.v.**) that is venerated, especially in the annual haj or pilgrimage. In Medina it is the Prophet Mohammad's mosque where the founder of the Islamic religion is buried. Non-believers are not allowed to enter Mecca or Medina. In Jerusalem it is the Temple Mount (**q.v.**).

homosexual The word applies to both men and women, not just to men. Therefore do not write *homosexuals and lesbians* although you can refer to *homosexual men and women*.

Hong Kong   Founded as a British colony in 1841, Hong Kong reverts to Beijing's sovereignty as a Special Administrative Region (SAR) of the People's Republic of China on July 1, 1997. Hong Kong's 5.6 million population, mainly Chinese, was never consulted. China has guaranteed to preserve Hong Kong's economic, social and legal set-up for 50 years under the "one country, two systems" concept promoted by Chinese paramount leader Deng Xiaoping.

hopefully   For centuries *hopefully* simply meant *with hope*. Recently it has become a vogue word meaning *it is hoped that. . . .*Stick to the original meaning unless quoting someone.

horde, hoard   A *horde* is a *multitude*, a *hoard* is a *hidden stock* or *treasure*.

howitzer   An artillery piece with a relatively short barrel designed to fire at a high angle over hills. See **weapons**.

HUD   Department of Housing and Urban Development (U.S.).

hundredweight   U.K./U.S. long = 112 pounds/50.8 kilograms. U.S. short = 100 pounds/45.4 kilograms. See also **measures**.

hung   See **hang**.

hurricanes   See **storms**.

hyphenated titles   When a hyphenated title is capitalised, capitalise both parts, e.g. *Lieutenant-General John Smith, U.N. Secretary-General Boutros Boutros-Ghali.*

hyphenation   See **punctuation**.

I

IAEA International Atomic Energy Agency (Vienna).

IATA International Air Transport Association (Geneva).

ibn Use *bin* in Arab names to mean *son of*.

IBRD International Bank for Reconstruction and Development (World Bank).

ICAO International Civil Aviation Organisation (Montreal).

ICBM Intercontinental ballistic missile.

ICO See **OIC**.

ICRC International Committee of the Red Cross (Geneva). See **Red Cross**.

Id al-Adha, Id al-Fitr See **Eid al-Adha, Eid al-Fitr**.

idiosyncrasy Not *idiosyncracy*.

IISS International Institute for Strategic Studies (London).

ilk A word almost universally misused in phrases like *social climbers and people of that ilk* (intended to mean *people of that kind*). The phrase you want is simply *social climbers and people like that*. The phrase *of that ilk* can be correctly used only of a Scottish laird's territorial possessions. *Hamish Glengarry of that Ilk* would mean *Hamish Glengarry who owned an estate of the same name, i.e. Glengarry*.

ILO International Labour Organisation (Geneva).

IMCO Inter-Governmental Maritime Consultative Organisation (London).

IMF International Monetary Fund (Washington). A specialised agency of the U.N. which provides funds to member countries under certain conditions of need and commitments of policy. The funds are usually for short-term purposes, especially balance of payments. Its main units are the policy-making Interim Committee and the Development Committee.

imply, infer   A speaker or writer *implies* by insinuating or suggesting indirectly. A listener or reader *infers* by drawing a conclusion from what is said.

impresario   Not *impressario*.

in the event of   Avoid this clumsy bureaucratic phrase. Write *If war should break out. . . .* or *Should war break out . . .* not *In the event of war. . . .*

inch   To convert roughly to centimetres multiply by 5 and divide by 2; to convert precisely multiply by 2.54.

index   Use *indices* as the plural when the word is used to mean a measurement of economic activity, *indexes* in other senses.

India   See **Assam, Kashmir, Punjab**.

indicated   Best avoided as it implies subjective interpretation by the journalist.

indirect speech   Write *He said he would act* not *He said he will act*. The exception is in a lead paragraph with the source at the end – *Finland will sign a trade agreement next week with the three Baltic republics, its prime minister said on Tuesday*.

industrial action   Avoid this euphemism. If you mean a strike, say so.

infer   See **imply**.

inflation   Persistent upward movement in the general price level together with a subsequent, related drop in purchasing power. Normally shorthand for the annual rate of increase in consumer prices, but it can refer, for example, to wholesale prices or wages. We report the percentage increase in the official price index over the previous month and over the same month of the previous year (the annual rate). The annualised rate of inflation, less commonly used, is the process of taking a figure for part of the year and extrapolating it to obtain a figure for the whole year.

injuries, wounds   *Wounds* are sustained in combat or by gunfire, axe blow, knifing, etc. *Injuries* are received in falls, car crashes and the like. Be as specific as possible, e.g. *He broke his right leg* not *He* *broke a leg.* Avoid hospitalese. Write *He broke his left arm* not *He sustained an arm fracture.*

Inmarsat   A global satellite operator based in London with more than 60 member countries which provides maritime, land mobile and aeronautical communications. Originally International Maritime Satellite Organisation.

Inmarsat-A   An Inmarsat satellite communications system which can handle duplex voice, picture and data traffic via a terminal that fits into one or two large suitcases.

Inmarsat-C   An Inmarsat satellite system which handles slow-speed half-duplex communications for text only. Originally dubbed the "shoe-box terminal", because it is intended to create truly portable miniaturised equipment that fits into a brief-case.

innocent   Report a plea as it was made in court. If it was *not guilty*, do not report it as *innocent.*

inquiry   Not *enquiry.*

insider trading   Journalists handling economic news stories should be aware that insider trading and tipping are a criminal offence in many countries to which heavy penalties are attached. The following guidelines are based upon U.S. law, which is perhaps the most stringent of any country's on this issue.

Insider trading is the buying or selling of the securities of any company (including your own) while in possession of material, non-public information about it. Tipping is the improper disclosure of such information.

Put simply, you would be guilty of insider trading or tipping if, while possessing information about a company that is not in the public domain, you bought or sold securities or gave to a third party information on the basis of which they bought, sold or retained securities.

Information is considered material if it is likely to affect the market price of a security and there is a substantial likelihood that a reasonable investor would attach importance to it in deciding whether to buy, sell or hold a security. It is irrelevant whether the information is factual or speculative.

Examples of material information include information about contemplated mergers or acquisitions, impending bankruptcy, business plans, proposed sale or purchase of assets, pending government reports and statistics, e.g. the consumer price index, financial forecasts, earnings estimates, changes in management and the gain or loss of a substantial customer or supplier.

Information is considered non-public until it has been publicly disclosed (in a major news publication or wire service, in a public filing made to a regulatory agency or in materials sent to shareholders) and the market has had enough time to absorb and react to the information. It should be assumed that information obtained in the course of your employment is non-public. The fact that rumours about this information may be circulating, even if they are widespread, does not mean that the information is public and does not relieve you from the obligation to treat the information as non-public.

If you wish to keep on the right side of the law, do not buy or sell securities of any company, including your own, while possessing ·material, non-public information about that company, whether or not it has been obtained through your work, and do not recommend or suggest that anyone else, including family and friends, buy, sell or retain the securities of any company, including your own, while possessing such material, non-public information.

insolvency   See **bankruptcy**.

install   Not *instal*. *Installation* but *instalment*.

instil   *instilled*. *Instillation* but *instilment*.

insure   See **ensure**.

Intelsat   The International Telecommunications Satellite Consortium (Washington), which has more than 100 member nations.

International Bank for Reconstruction and Development   The full name of the World Bank in Washington. *World Bank* can be used as an alternative short form.

International Court of Justice   This is the proper title of the World Court in The Hague, which is the main U.N. judicial body. Always use the term *World Court* at second reference.

Interpol   The International Criminal Police Organisation (Paris). Use *Interpol* at all references.

interpretation   All stories should be written so that the significance of the events or words reported is immediately clear to the reader. This must be done without compromising accuracy, balance or sourcing.

Quotes from people with vigorous opinions can be woven in to make a lively, even provocative story without expressing, either directly or by the use of loaded words, a value judgment or forecast. Named sources should be used wherever possible. If this cannot be done, explain the nature of the sources you are quoting as specifically as possible, e.g. *Arab diplomats who attended the meeting said. . . .*

Where such comment is not immediately available, background information can be used to put a development in context and thus make clear its significance.

See also **sourcing**.

intifada   The Palestinian uprising against the Israeli occupation of East Jerusalem, the West Bank and the Gaza Strip, which began on December 9, 1987.

invoke   See **evoke**.

IOC   International Olympic Committee (Lausanne).

IOM   International Organisation for Migration (Geneva). This is a non-U.N. inter-governmental agency whose main task is to arrange the movement of refugees and migrants to new homes. In early 1992 there were 43 countries with full membership and a further 30 with observer status.

IPTC format   The International Press Telecommunications Council has an alternative sequence of prefatory information about stories to that of ANPA (**q.v.**). Unlike the American system it allows for national variations. Information such as story number, date and time, priority, category code and keyword is placed in predetermined fields.

IRA   Irish Republican Army. May be used alone at first reference from a dateline in the British Isles. The IRA split in 1969 when the IRA Army Council voted by three to one to give token recognition to three parliaments – in London, Dublin and Belfast. This proved too much for those who had always backed a violent campaign to drive the British from Northern Ireland. The movement split into the Provisional IRA, the prime mover behind the violence ever since, and the Official IRA. The OIRA has been largely inactive since 1972 when it declared a ceasefire. See also **Northern Ireland**.

Ireland   Do not use *Eire* for the Republic of Ireland. See *Northern Ireland*.

Irian Jaya   The Indonesian name for West New Guinea.

ironically   A word that should be used with great care as it is so often used incorrectly.

IRS   Internal Revenue Service (U.S.).

-isation, ization and -ise, -ize   House styles vary but the preference is increasingly for the forms *-isation* and *ise*.

ISO   The International Standards Organisation (Geneva), the authority on international standards in, among others, computing and manufacturing.

Israeli names   Use *ch* rather than *h* in transliterating Israeli names into English, e.g. *Chaim* not *Haim*. Use the *h* form only if you know that this is the individual's personal preference.

IT   Information technology.

its, it's   The possessive pronoun has no apostrophe, unlike the contraction *it's* meaning *it is*.

IWC   International Whaling Commission (Cambridge, England).

J

Jamahiriyah The official name of Libya is the Socialist People's Libyan Arab Jamahiriyah. *Jamahiriyah*, which means *state of the masses*, sometimes appears alone in copy from Libya. Use *Libya* or, if the word is in quotation, use a form like *The radio said the Jamahiriyah (Libya) would.* . . .

Jap Do not use as an abbreviation for Japanese, except in quotation.

jargon The general principles stated by H.W. and F.G. Fowler 80 years ago hold good:

Prefer the familiar word to the far-fetched.

Prefer the short word to the long and the single word to the circumlocution.

Prefer the concrete word to the abstract.

Prefer the Saxon word to the Romance.

To expand on Fowler, avoid pompous words like *ongoing, escalating, prestigious, meaningful.*

More often than not you can also do without *special, key, dramatic, major, giant, large-scale, massive* and *crisis.*

Modish words like *confrontation* substitute polysyllabic vagueness for the crisp precision of (in this case) *clash, dispute* or even *war.*

If you have to convert into better English words like *confrontation,* use the most conservative and unambiguous of its various meanings.

Political and military jargon is riddled with euphemism and serves as much to conceal as to express meaning. Unless you are directly quoting someone, turn jargon into clear English.

Avoid stilted expressions like *at this moment . . . in respect of . . . in receipt of . . . with a view to . . . attributable to . . . owing to an excess of . . . in connection with . . . are availing themselves of . . . have made available . . . remuneration . . . (de)escalation . . . methodology . . . in the wake of . . . apprehension as to the outcome.*

See also **cliches, long words**.

Jeddah Not *Jedda* or *Jiddah*, Saudi Arabia.

jehad Use *jihad* (**q.v.**) for an Islamic holy war.

Jerusalem The status of the city is disputed by Israelis and Arabs. Do not use it as a synonym for Israel, as in *the Jerusalem government*.

jets Most modern airliners and military aircraft have jet engines. Avoid such terms as *jet airliner* or *jetliner* unless the fact that the aircraft is jet-powered is relevant. It would be more helpful to specify if an airliner or military aircraft were piston-engined.

Jew Use for both men and women. Do not use *Jewess*.

jewelry Use *jewellery*.

journalese Words and phrases that grow stale with repetition are cliches. Journalese comprises cliches beloved of journalists and often stems from the importing back into the text of language used as shorthand in headlines. Some examples to avoid: *amid reports that . . . brace for a wave of violence . . . burgeoning* (growing) *. . . cutback* (cut) *. . . economic/fiscal woes . . . embattled . . . giant* (large) *. . . global* (unless you mean literally that) *. . . hit by fears that . . . in a bid to hammer out agreement . . . lash out . . . longtime foe . . . looks set to . . . major* (big, large) *. . . massive* (big) *. . . meaningful* (real, significant) *. . . modalities* (means, procedures) *. . . mum* (silent) *. . . ok's* (approves) *. . . oil-rich . . . parameters* (limits) *. . . probe* (inquiry) *. . . reportedly . . . rocked by . . . the statement came as . . . war-torn.*

judgment Not *judgement*.

judo, ju-jitsu *judo* is a modern form of *ju-jitsu*, Japanese wrestling.

jumbo jet Loosely a large wide-bodied airliner, specifically the Boeing 747.

junta A political clique or a government formed by such a clique, usually after a revolution.

K

Kaaba Islam's most sacred shrine at the centre of the great mosque in Mecca. It is a mass of stone 38 feet high, 40 long and 30 wide (11×12×9 metres). See **Holy Places**.

Kampuchea Use *Cambodia*, except in quotation.

Kashmir A Himalayan region whose Hindu rajah signed a treaty of accession to India on partition of the sub-continent in 1947 when faced with a revolt in West Kashmir. Pathans from Pakistan intervened and the two countries fought over the state in 1947–48. A U.N.-brokered ceasefire agreement in 1949 left about one third of the state in the hands of Pakistan, which refers to it as Azad (Free) Kashmir. Jammu and Kashmir, the Indian section, is India's only Moslem-majority state. A simmering anti-Indian mood in Jammu and Kashmir exploded into a separatist campaign in January 1990 after militants kidnapped a minister's daughter and the government traded her for five jailed secessionists. The state was placed under direct rule from Delhi. Several dozen groups are fighting for a re-united and independent Kashmir or to join Pakistan. Two of the three Indo-Pakistan wars have been over Kashmir, and Delhi accuses Islamabad of arming and training the separatists. Pakistan denies the charge. Delhi also sees Islamic fundamentalism behind the uprising, but most Kashmiri Moslems say it is nationalist. Indian security forces have been widely accused of murder, torture, rape and burning homes, most of which the government denies.

Kathmandu Not *Katmandu*, Nepal.

kerosene Not *kerosine*. Medium-light distillate used for lighting and heating and to provide fuel for jet and turbo-prop aircraft engines. Called *paraffin* or *paraffin oil* in the United Kingdom.

KGB (Soviet) Committee for State Security. *Soviet KGB* is acceptable at first reference, with an explanation lower in the story that KGB means the (former) Soviet security police or service

Khmer Rouge ˙ Chinese-backed Cambodian Communists. See **Cambodia**.

kibbutz   Plural *kibbutzim*. An Israeli collective settlement.

kilogram   Use *kg* (no full stop, same singular and plural) at all references. Convert kilograms to pounds for small weights (below 1,000 kg), to tons for larger weights. To convert roughly to pounds multiply by 22 and divide by 10, precisely multiply by 2.205. To convert roughly to tons divide by 1,000, precisely multiply by 0.000984.

kilometre   Use *km* (no full stop, same singular and plural) at all references, except in a phrase like *hundreds of kilometres*. To convert roughly to miles multiply by 5 and divide by 8, precisely multiply by 0.621.

kiloton   A measure of explosive force, equal to that of 1,000 tons of TNT. The atomic bomb dropped at Hiroshima on August 6, 1945, was a 12.5-kiloton weapon.

king   At second reference either *the king* or the full name, e.g. *King Baudouin*. Do not capitalise the titles of deposed monarchs, e.g. *ex-king Zahir Shah*.

Kiribati   Formerly Gilbert Islands, West Pacific.

knot   A measurement of speed, not distance. It tells you how many nautical miles (1.15 statute miles) a vessel or aircraft has travelled in one hour. Do not convert to miles per hour. Do not write *knots per hour*.

Korean names   Koreans put the surname first, followed by the given name, normally hyphenated, e.g. *Kim Dae-jung*, but sometimes as one word, e.g. *Moon Ihlwan*. In both cases the second half of the given name is lower case. Some Koreans have two- or three-word names, unhyphenated, e.g. *Chun Doo Hwan*. Use the surname only at second reference, e.g. *Kim, Chun*.

L

laager, lager A *laager* is a defensive encampment, literally or metaphorically, while *lager* is a beer.

lady Use *woman.*

lakh In India *100,000.* Explain if used.

LAN Local area network, grouping a number of pieces of equipment, typically PCs, printers, modems, faxes, database machines, etc.

Land One of the federal states comprising Germany or Austria. Plural *Laender.*

landline A terrestrial, as opposed to a satellite, communications link.

Laos Use *Lao* for the language. Otherwise the adjective is *Laotian,* although there is a Lao ethnic group.

large-scale *big* is shorter and usually better.

laser Acronym for a device using light amplification by stimulated emission of radiation, used in microsurgery and high-technology industry.

lathi Heavy stick carried by Indian police. Explain if used.

latter, last It is *the latter* of two things, *the last* of more than two things.

LCD Liquid crystal display.

leads A lead can be simply a synonym for an intro – the opening paragraph of a news story. In news agencies it is also a term for a fresh story that carries an earlier report forward by weaving together new developments, and often fresh interpretation, with material already on the file to give readers an up-to-date and comprehensive "wrap" of all significant information available at the time of writing.

You normally begin a lead with the latest development or by

twinning this with the key point from the earlier story. But this is not necessarily the case. If a new development is less important than the angle at the top of the existing story, it can be incorporated lower in the lead. There is no obligation to change the wording of the lead paragraph of such a story if it is not outdated by the new development.

Be careful to preserve the natural word order for the time elements in leads, e.g. *Police on Monday arrested two men trying to smuggle drugs* . . . not *Police arrested two men on Monday trying to smuggle drugs.* . . .

lead paragraphs   These are the most important part of any story so it is worth taking time over them. Those first 20 or 30 words make or break the story. If they do not seize the reader's attention or imagination, the story is dead.

The programmatic lead, reporting the surface activity that has taken place or is planned rather than digging into the essence of the story, is the kiss of death. No prizes for saying which is the better of these leads run by rival news agencies on an international conference:

1. *Senior officials put the final touches to the agenda for the Commonwealth summit on Monday as leaders poured into Harare for Wednesday's opening of the week-long conference.*

2. *Deprived of apartheid as their focus, leaders of the 50-nation Commonwealth of Britain and its ex-colonies meet this week with attention turned on a once-taboo subject – their own often chequered human rights records.*

Ideally a lead paragraph should be able to stand as a self-contained story, complete with source if the subject is contentious. Do not clutter leads with detail, long titles or pinpoint geography. As a general rule a lead paragraph should not run to more than about 30 words.

See also **soft leads**.

leave   Avoid limp phrases like *The fire left six people dead* or *The strike left housewives angry*. Fires do not leave people dead, they kill them. Strikes anger housewives, not leave them angry.

Lebanon   Not *the Lebanon*.

left wing   *a left-winger, a left-wing politician*, but *the left wing* of the political spectrum.

legally risky stories You should draw to the attention of your editor stories that may be legally dangerous so that a decision on whether to publish can be taken at a senior level. See also **contempt of court, libel**.

lend, loan Use *lend* rather than *loan* as a verb.

Leningrad Now again *St Petersburg*, second city of Russia and the former tsarist capital.

less than, fewer Use *fewer* when referring to numbers of individual items, *less* for quantities.

level *levelled.*

leu Romanian unit of currency. Plural *lei.*

leukaemia Not *leukemia.*

libel Defamation, a slur on the good name of an individual, a group of people or a commercial company, is the most common legal risk journalists have to guard against. The laws are complex, varying from country to country. Take no chances. If you consider a story may be defamatory draw your editor's attention to it and, if appropriate, explain your reservations.

Under English law a story may be considered libellous if it exposes a plaintiff to hatred, ridicule or contempt; if it lowers them in the estimation of right-thinking members of society; or if it disparages them in office, profession or trade.

In defence of a libel action one may argue that the story is true, constitutes fair comment on a matter of public interest, is privileged (i.e. protected by law) or contains unintentional defamation. A fair, accurate and contemporaneous court report, for instance, is normally privileged. A plea of unintentional defamation would be easier to argue if your newspaper had issued an immediate correction of the offending story.

Guard against action for libel by giving anyone maligned in a story an opportunity to reply, ideally in the same story but if not then as soon as possible thereafter.

Be precise in specifying the name, age, home address and occupation of an accused.

It is no defence against a libel action to omit the name of the person maligned or to qualify the words complained of with *an alleged*.

Some countries take a fairly relaxed view of defamation, but remember that a plaintiff may seek redress in another country with stricter laws, such as Britain.

Reporters and correspondents should keep for at least two years notes and tapes on which they have based a story that might be legally sensitive.

See also **legally risky stories**.

Libor   London Interbank Offered Rate. See **bonds**.

Libya   See **Jamahiriyah**.

licence, license   *licence* is the noun, *license* the verb.

lieutenant   Hyphenate *lieutenant-colonel* and *lieutenant-commander*. At second reference just *the colonel, the commander. second lieutenant* is not hyphenated but *sub-lieutenant* is. In the U.S. navy it is *Lieutenant (j.g.) John Smith, j.g.* meaning *junior grade.*

LIFFE   The London International Financial Futures Exchange, the London market for futures contracts.

light-year   A measure of distance not time. It is the distance light travels in one year, about six million million miles or 9.6 million million km.

like   Except in quotation, do not use *like* to mean *as if*, e.g. *He was spending money like there was no tomorrow.*

linchpin   Not *lynchpin*. But *lynch law*.

liquefy   Not *liquify*. But *liquidate*.

liquidation See **bankruptcy**.

lira Italian unit of currency. Plural *lire*.

literally Use with great care. People using this word in fact almost always mean metaphorically, e.g. *He was literally shattered* or *He was literally over the moon.*

litre To convert roughly to Imperial gallons multiply by 2 and divide by 9, precisely multiply by 0.22.
  To convert roughly to U.S. gallons divide by 4, precisely multiply by 0.264.

Lloyd's The London association of underwriters. Note apostrophe. Lloyds Bank has no apostrophe.

loans Do not use the verb *give* when referring to loans; they are paid for through interest. *Make* or *issue* is better. To avoid confusion, do not say someone is *raising* a loan when it is being arranged. Use the word *raise* only when the amount of a loan already arranged is being increased.
  In business page stories you should give the exact name of the borrower, whether the loan is being guaranteed by a parent company or another body, the amount, the maturity and the interest rate.
  If the interest rate is variable or "floating", give the specific reference or base rate of interest, e.g. the three-month or six-month London interbank offered rate (Libor), and the margin on interest paid above, or even below it, e.g. *1/4 point.*
  Abbreviations like *Libor, Sibor*, etc., are fine on second reference or in headlines.
  The interest payment might vary with the maturity. A five-year loan could pay 1/8 over Libor for three years, rising to 1/4 over Libor for the last two years.
  The loan might have a grace period – the period during which only interest and no principal is paid.

long words As a general rule use short words rather than long. Here are some long words commonly and unnecessarily used when there is an acceptable shorter version.

additional	more	attempt	try
alternative	other	confrontation	clash, dispute
approximately	about	construct	build

cutback	cut	large-scale	big
demonstrate	show	manufacture	make
dispatch	send	meaningful	real
discover	find	modalities	means
donate	give	negotiations	talks
escalate, escalation	rise, increase	numerous	many
establish	set up	participate	take part
exponential	rapid	permit	let
extinguish	put out	purchase	buy
facility	plant, base	requirements	needs
finalise	complete	sufficient	enough
following	after	transportation	transport

Lord's   The London cricket ground. Note apostrophe.

low-income   If you mean *poor*, say so.

LNG   liquefied natural gas.

LPG   liquefied petroleum gas (mainly propane and butane).

LSD   Lysergic acid diethylamide, the hallucinogenic drug. The initials may be used alone at all references.

LSE   London School of Economics.

lunar new year   The Chinese and some Southeast Asian people have a 12-year lunar new year cycle, with each year assigned an animal zodiac sign in strict rotation. For the Chinese the cycle is *Rat, Ox, Tiger, Rabbit, Dragon, Snake, Horse, Goat, Monkey, Rooster, Dog* and *Pig*. Certain qualities are attributed to each year, depending on the animal sign. For example, anyone born in the Year of the Pig is considered generous and prosperous. Such a year would see prosperity in business for all.

The holiday lasts three days and is seen as a time to repay all debts and get a haircut and a new set of clothes, signifying a fresh start. Firecrackers play a noisy part in new year festivities.

In Vietnam the lunar new year holiday is known as *Tet*. The Communist Tet offensive in South Vietnamese cities in 1968 marked a turning point in the Vietnam war.

Luxembourg   Not *Luxemburg*.

Lyon   Not *Lyons*, France.

M

Macao Use *Macau*.

machinegun One word as noun and verb. Use *machinegun* for fully automatic weapons mounted on a support, normally with a calibre of .303 upwards. The standard infantry weapon, like the Kalashnikov or M-16, although often loosely called a machinegun, is in fact an assault rifle or automatic rifle and usually has a smaller calibre. See also **weapons**.

Madagascar Use *Malagasy* for the people and the language.

magazine titles House styles vary but usually the title is not italicised or put in quotes. Whatever the formal (masthead) title, capitalise only adjectives and nouns, e.g. *an article in the New Yorker*.

Maghreb Loosely North Africa, less Egypt, and literally the western part of the Middle East. The Arab Maghreb Union, a political and economic alliance, was created in February 1989 of Morocco, Mauritania, Algeria, Tunisia and Libya to face the challenge of the single European market planned for 1992. Maghreb is also the official name in Arabic of the Moroccan state.

maintain Use this word with care. Like *claim* it suggests that you are sceptical about the statement quoted.

major A much overused adjective. Find a more precise alternative.

Malagasy The people or language of Madagascar.

Maldive Islands Adjective *Maldivian*, South Asia.

Mali Adjective *Malian*, West Africa.

manageable Not *managable*.

manifesto *manifestos*.

manoeuvre Not *maneuvre* or *maneuver*.

marijuana See **drugs**.

mark   The German currency. The full name, not normally used, is *deutschemark*.

marquis   Not *marquess*.

Marseille   Not *Marseilles*, France.

marshal   Not *marshall* as noun or verb. Past tense of verb *marshalled*. But the *Marshall Plan* and the *Marshall Islands* in the Pacific.

Massawa   Not *Massoua*, Ethiopia.

materiel   Use the English term *military equipment*.

may, can   See **can, may**.

mayoress   The wife of a mayor, not a woman mayor.

MCAs   Monetary compensatory amounts are the subsidies and taxes that even up prices across the European Community to take account of fluctuations in exchange rates.

McDonald's   The hamburger chain.

McDonnell Douglas Corp   Not *MacDonnell* for the U.S. aircraft company.

measures   When abbreviating metric units use the singular form without a full stop, e.g. *kg* or *km* not *kgs* or *kms*.
  The following need not be spelled out on first mention: *kg, km, lb, cm, mm*.
  See also **conversions, ton/tonne**.

Médecins sans Frontières   Literally *Doctors without Frontiers*, a Paris-based group of volunteer doctors and other medical staff of various nationalities who operate with the agreement of the local government in any situation where they are needed, e.g. war, epidemics, famine. It has no political line.

media   A plural noun.

medical stories   Handle stories about new threats to health or reputed cures for AIDS, cancer and other scourges with great care. They play on the hopes and fears of millions of people.
  If you have any doubts about such a story or are unfamiliar with the subject, draw it to the attention of your editor, explaining how you got the story, the strength of your source and the checks you have made. If a story making dramatic claims for a cure for AIDS or

cancer does not come from a reputable named source it should be checked with recognised medical experts before being issued (or

spiked). If such a story is issued it should include whatever balancing or interpretative material is available from such authorities.

mediaeval Not *medieval*.

meet *He met party leaders* not *He met with party leaders*.

megaton A measure of explosive force. A megaton is equivalent to the explosive force of one million tons of TNT (trinitrotoluene).

Melanesia An island group in the Southwest Pacific. Micronesia is a group north of Melanesia and Polynesia is in the central Pacific.

Mercalli scale See **earthquakes**.

Mercedes-Benz Note hyphen.

Messerschmitt Not *Messerschmidt* for the German aircraft or in the aerospace and armaments group Messerschmitt-Boelkow-Bloehm.

metaphors A fresh and vivid metaphor can add much to a story. But avoid mixed metaphors, e.g. *The Egyptian swimmers walked away with the championships*, and metaphors whose literal sense is absurd e.g. *a growing bottleneck* – which, if you think about it, should solve rather than aggravate a problem.

metre Convert metres to feet for short distances (up to 10 metres), to yards for longer distances.
  To convert roughly to feet add a zero and divide by 3; to convert precisely multiply by 3.28.
  To convert roughly to yards add a zero and divide by 9; to convert precisely multiply by 1.094.

Micronesia   See **Melanesia**.

Middle Eastern currencies   Saudi riyal, Kuwaiti dinar, Qatar riyal, Omani rial, Iranian rial, Iraqi dinar, UAE dirham and Bahrain dinar.

These are the official names of the currencies concerned as notified to the International Monetary Fund by the respective countries. Note the difference between the riyal and the rial.

MiG   Use this abbreviation for the Soviet aircraft, e.g. *MiG-25*.

milage   Use *mileage*.

mile   To convert roughly to kilometres multiply by 8 and divide by 5, precisely multiply by 1.609. One nautical or sea mile equals 1.853 km.

millennium   Not *millenium*. Plural is *millennia*.

million   Unless your house style specifies the abbreviations **mln** or *m*. spell it out in full.

millimetre   Abbrevation *mm* (no full stop, same singular and plural), acceptable at all references.

miniscule   Use *minuscule* if you wish to describe something very small.

minister   *French Foreign Minister Roland Dumas* but *Roland Dumas, the French foreign minister . . . The minister said. . . .*

ministry   *the German Defence Ministry* or *the Defence Ministry said on Friday German troops would. . . .* But *the French and German defence ministries* and *the ministry said. . . .*

miracles   Keep miracles for religious stories, and then refer to such only when quoting a source. In disaster reports avoid the seemingly obligatory cliche *"It was a miracle no one was killed," said a rescue worker.*

MIRV   Acceptable at first reference for multiple independently targetable re-entry vehicle. Copy should explain that each of the warheads carried by this intercontinental ballistic missile can be aimed at a different target.

misplaced phrases   Misplacing a phrase in a sentence can make it absurd, even libellous, e.g. *The magazine ran an article about adultery* *by the Archbishop of Canterbury* when what is meant is *The magazine ran an article by the Archbishop of Canterbury about adultery.* When re-reading your copy keep an eye out for such egregious errors.

MIT   Massachusetts Institute of Technology, Cambridge, Mass.

mob   Use this word with care and never of a political protest. The neutral *crowd* is usually better unless there is an outbreak of unorganised violence.

modalities   Jargon. It is better to use a word like *means* or *procedures*.

modem   Modulator-demodulator, a device that enables computers, etc., to talk to one another over telecommunications channels. Modems conform either to CCITT or Bell standards.

Moldova   The name by which the government of the former Moldavia now styles the former Soviet republic.

Monaco   Not *Monte Carlo* as a dateline.

mongol   Do not use *mongol* or *mongoloid* to refer to sufferers from Down's syndrome, a form of mental retardation caused by the improper splitting of chromosomes during gestation. In subsequent references it is acceptable to refer to the adjective being commonly used because of the eye-shape, which is a noticeable symptom.

Mont Blanc   At 15,771 feet/4,807 metres, this French mountain is the highest in western Europe. The highest mountain in Europe is Elbrus (18,498 feet/5,642 metres) in the Caucasus.

moot   Little understood outside the United States. If you use the phrase *a moot point* in a quote, explain it – *a debatable point*.

mortar   A mortar is a weapon from which a bomb (not a shell) is fired. *The trench was mortared* and *Mortar bombs fell on the trench* are correct. *Mortars fell on the trench* is not.

mosquito   *mosquitoes*.

mpg, mph   *miles per gallon, miles per hour* – both acceptable at all references, both lower case and without full stops.

mount   Write in full, whether of mountains or communities, e.g. *Mount Everest, Mount Vernon*.

move to   This phrase is frequently used to give a spurious sense of physical action when in fact the only action has been verbal, e.g. *Bush moved to head off congressional opposition to his budget plans when he said. . . .* Avoid it.

MRCA   multi-role combat aircraft.

mujahideen   A term for Islamic guerrilla groups, meaning *holy warriors*.

multilateral, multinational   Both one word.

multiplexer (MUX)   A device to enable a number of signals to share the same physical transmission channel, using frequency division multiplexing (FDM), time division multiplexing (TDM) or statistical multiplexing (statmux).

Muslim   Use *Moslem* except for the *Black Muslims* in the United States.

Myanmar   See **Burma**.

N

NAACP National Association for the Advancement of Coloured People (U.S.).

names See **personal names**.

names and titles Avoid clumsy strings of names and titles. *Foreign Minister Hans Dietrich Genscher* is fine. *Under-Secretary for Military Procurement Major-General Abdul Razzak* is not. Split up such names and titles; either *the Under-Secretary for Military Procurement, Major-General Abdul Razzak,* or *Major-General Abdul Razzak, under-secretary for military procurement.*

Nanjing Not *Nanking*, China.

naphtha Not *naptha.*

NASA National Aeronautics and Space Administration (U.S.). At first reference a form like *the U.S. space agency NASA* is acceptable.

National Guard Explain in copy that this is a U.S. militia force.

national names You need not specify a minister's nationality in the first paragraph of a story under the dateline naming that nation. Under a Washington dateline, for example, write: *Secretary of State James Baker said on Friday the United States would . . .* not *United States Secretary of State James Baker said on Friday the United States would. . . .*

There is likewise no need to specify the nationality of groups that are obviously of the nationality of the country datelined. So under an Athens dateline write *Police arrested . . .* not *Greek police arrested. . . .*

nationality and race Capitalise words denominating nationality, race or language, e.g. *Arab, African, Argentine, Caucasian, Chinese, Eskimo, Finnish.*

nationwide Rarely necessary in the phrase *nationwide broadcast.* If a head of state or government goes on television or radio we can assume the broadcast is nationwide.

NATO   North Atlantic Treaty Organisation (Brussels). The initials may be used by themselves at first reference with the full name given lower in the story. Members in 1992: Belgium, Britain, Canada, Denmark, France, Germany, Greece, Iceland, Italy, Luxembourg, the Netherlands, Norway, Portugal, Spain, Turkey and the United States. France withdrew from NATO's integrated military structure in 1966 but remains a member of the alliance.

nautical mile   1,852 metres or 1.1515 statute miles. Do not convert the nautical mile used for fishing limits, by ships when reporting distances at sea and by NASA and others reporting space shots. If using nautical miles in space stories, make this clear in text. See also **knot**.

NCB   National Coal Board (U.K.).

negro   Use *black* in a U.S. context. Plural *negroes*. Do not use *negress*.

neither . . . nor   Use when referring to two elements only, e.g. *Neither Norway nor Sweden voted*. Do not write *Neither Norway, Sweden nor Denmark voted*. If both elements are singular use a singular verb, e.g. *Neither France nor Germany welcomes the prospect*. If it gets more complicated, e.g. *Neither the players nor the referee is/are fit*, it's best to recast the sentence. Never write *neither . . . or. . . .*

not . . .nor   It is increasingly common to see such incorrect forms as *He did not like football nor cricket* or *Israel will never talk directly with the PLO nor recognise their legitimacy*. The only negative particle after which you should use *nor* is *neither*.

Nepali   Not *Nepalese* as adjective.

Netherlands   In text write *the Netherlands*, in datelines omit the article, e.g. *ARNHEM, Netherlands, May 16. . . .*

neutral verbs   The verb *to say* is usually the best, neutral choice in reporting a speech or statement. *Alleged, claimed* or *maintained* could imply that you do not believe a statement while *noted, pointed out* or *emphasised* suggest that you do.

Use *announced* with care. Only competent authorities have the right to make announcements.

Avoid *concede* which implies an admission of guilt or previous error. Prefer *acknowledge*.

Do not write *refute* (which means *disprove*) when you mean no more than *deny* or *reject*.

Other potentially partisan verbs to avoid include *admitted, asserted, affirmed, contended, stressed, suggested*.

new Companies often announce that they will build a new plant. *New* is superfluous since, by definition, any plant being built must be new.

news analyses The news analysis, under whatever name it appears, is a vital component of a serious newspaper. Its purpose is simple – to explain the significance of an event, to trace its origins and, where possible, to indicate how the story might develop.

Normally any story of substance should contain an element of analysis and where possible straight news coverage and analysis should be wrapped together into a single story or lead, with the news and the views clearly distinguished.

A separate news analysis may be called for if the news development is very important or complex or if there is a significant gap between the time when a news event is first reported and when it is possible to gather the information needed for a coherent analysis of its significance.

A news analysis should restate the key new elements in the story it is coupled to but the emphasis must be on interpretation and explanation, avoiding statements of the obvious. Do not simply rehash a news story with a few lines of comment.

Analysis should be derived where possible from named sources in a position to speak with informed knowledge on the issue. Failing that, it should draw on unattributable sources whose orientation is made as clear as possible so that the reader can assess their possible degree of bias. In the absence of immediate comment from qualified sources on a news development, it is still possible to write a useful news analysis by putting the news in context of previous events and listing possible explanations for what has happened and scenarios for what might happen next.

news conference Use this phrase rather than *press conference* with its implied exclusion of the non-print media.

news graphics News graphics enable newspapers with the necessary technical resources to portray both single events and trends with a depth and clarity that cannot be matched by either text or news pictures alone. News agency subscribers also call for a wide variety of artistic treatments of the news, e.g. flow charts, business graphs, three-dimensional cutaways, maps, plans and diagrams.

Newspapers differ in how their news graphics units massage the information they need. But a text journalist asked for input for a news graphic should be precise in detail – where exactly in Red Square the shot was fired, from which window on which floor on which side of a burning building did the woman throw herself, how many metres down and how many from the main shaft did the gas explode, along which runway and in which direction was the Boeing 747 taxiing when its fuselage was clipped by the landing gear of the DC-10 and on which runway and in which direction was the DC-10 landing?

Graphics artists may need to have faxed to them sections of relevant maps and also rough sketches (with a scale) of the scene of an incident on which they can build an accurate, detailed graphic.

When reporting statistics and trends for a graphic, highlights are rarely enough. Context is the key and you should provide all relevant figures so that the graphic can plot the movement of the trend and thus emphasise the new high or low point.

newspaper titles   House styles vary but normally there are no quotation marks around the title, which may or may not be italicised. Whatever the formal (masthead) title, capitalise only the adjectives and nouns, e.g. *an editorial in the New York Times* not *in The New York Times*. If a newspaper is well known, it is often not necessary to specify that it is a newspaper, e.g. *An editorial in the New York Times on Friday condemned . . .* is perfectly adequate.

nicknames   Treat .them as proper names when they refer to a specific person or thing, e.g. *the Iron Lady, the All Blacks, the Bermuda Triangle.*

no man's land   Not *no-man's-land.*

no one   Not *noone* or *no-one.*

nobility   The hereditary British nobility consists, in descending order of precedence, of dukes, marquises, earls, viscounts and barons. A few women are hereditary countesses or baronesses in their own right. Life peers, whose titles die with them, are also barons. The nobility are known collectively as peers (and peeresses), not lords, although the upper house of Parliament is the House of Lords.

Dukes get their full title at first reference, e.g. *the Duke of Norfolk*; second reference *Norfolk* or *the duke*. Never *Lord Norfolk*. His wife is *the Duchess of Norfolk* or *the duchess*, never *Lady Norfolk*.

We may refer to all other peers simply as *Lord So-and-So*, whatever their precise title, and to their wives as *Lady So-and-So*. However more formal titles may also be used if wished, e.g. *the Marquis of Zetland, Earl Cawdor, Viscount Boyd*. Barons, whether hereditary or life peers, are always *Lord So-and-So*. At second reference simply *So-and-So, Zetland, Cawdor, Boyd*.

The wife of an earl is a *countess*, of a viscount a *viscountess* and of a marquis a *marchioness*.

The children of dukes and marquises and the daughters of earls have the courtesy title of *lord* or *lady* before their first names. Do not use *the Honorable* or *the Hon.* before the names of the untitled sons of peers.

Baronets (whose titles are hereditary) and knights (whose titles die with them) are known as *Sir*, e.g. *Sir Reginald Barnett*. At second reference *Barnett*. However if you have to distinguish between him and his wife, use *Sir Reginald* and *Lady Barnett*. If he is a government minister the preferred style is *Sir Reginald Barnett, British health minister*, not *British Health Minister Sir Reginald Barnett*. His wife would be *Lady Barnett*, whether he was a baronet or a knight.

A dame, equivalent to a knight, is a woman honoured in her own right. At first reference *Dame Iris Murdoch*, then *Murdoch*.

See also **royalty**.

non- Hyphenate if the first element of a word is the negative *non-*, e.g. *a non-aggression pact*. But *nonconformist*.

Non-Aligned Movement Set up as a group of countries, mainly of the Third World, that were not aligned with either the United States or the Soviet Union. Its first summit was held in Belgrade in 1961. In 1992 it had 101 members. It has no permanent headquarters and its chairmanship rotates every three years.

non-conventional weapons Those that carry atomic, biological or chemical warheads. *Unconventional weapons* deliver high explosives by unconventional means.

none This may take either a singular or plural verb, although the singular form is more common.

non-existent Not *non-existant*.

non sequitur   Do not link two ideas that have no logical connection, e.g. *Jean Duval, who was married in Saigon in 1947, developed his new mousetrap out of an old shoe box.*

Nordic countries   Denmark, Finland, Iceland, Norway and Sweden. Scandinavia comprises only Denmark, Norway and Sweden. Because of the danger of confusion list the countries even if you use *Nordic* or *Scandinavian* in a lead for the sake of brevity.

normalcy   Use *normality*.

Northern Ireland   *Northern* is always upper case. Although Ulster is often used as a synonym, historically it includes two counties now in the Republic of Ireland. The Irish Republican Army, which is fighting to oust Britain from Northern Ireland, may be referred to by its initials alone at first reference from a dateline in the British Isles. Sinn Fein is its political wing.

For an international readership it is best to refer to the Northern Ireland conflict as a political and sectarian conflict. The IRA argue that they are freedom fighters not a sectarian organisation. Unless your house style decrees otherwise refer to them by such neutral terms as *guerrillas*, *gunmen* or *bombers*, depending on context. Use of the term *loyalist* for Protestant paramilitary or extremist groups is confusing for an international readership. Describe the Ulster Defence Regiment as *part-time British soldiers*.

See also **IRA**.

noted   You can *note* only established facts, not claims or opinions. Avoid the word.

nouns   See individual entries for nouns whose plural forms cause difficulties but observe these general rules:

-ey in the singular becomes *-eys* in the plural (*valley, valleys*)

-y becomes *-ies* (*baby, babies*)

-o becomes *-oes* in monosyllables and in the commoner two- and three-syllable words (*no, noes; hero, heroes; potato, potatoes*)

-o becomes *-os* in long words, proper names and abbreviations (*manifesto, manifestos; Tornado (aircraft), Tornados; photos, photo*)

Words with a vowel before the final *-o* become *-os* (*rodeo, rodeos; patio, patios; yahoo, yahoos; duo, duos*)

Many Anglicised foreign words keep their original plurals, e.g.:

addendum   addenda   beau   beaux

bureau	bureaux	minimum	minima
criterion	criteria	phenomenon	phenomena
memorandum	memoranda	plateau	plateaux

Note that *mediums* are clairvoyants while *media* are the means of mass communication; *series* does not change in the plural, *fish* generally remain fish but can be *fishes*; and *folk* usually remain *folk* except in colloquial phrases like *just plain folks*.

numbers   See **figures, fractions**.

numerous   *many* is shorter, better.

O

OAPEC Organisation of Arab Petroleum Exporting Countries (permanent headquarters in Kuwait although they were moved to Cairo temporarily after the Iraqi invasion in August 1990). Set up in 1968. Its 10 members in 1992 were Algeria, Bahrain, Egypt, Iraq, Kuwait, Libya, Qatar, Saudi Arabia, Syria and the United Arab Emirates.

OAS Organisation of American States (Washington). It has 35 active members representing all countries in the Americas except Cuba which was effectively expelled in 1962 but is still listed as a non-active member.

OAU Organisation of African Unity (Addis Ababa). All 52 African states except South Africa are members.

obscenities Follow your house rule on the use of obscenities. As a general rule they should be used only if they are in direct quotes and if the story would be seriously weakened by their omission. Obscenities, if retained, must not be euphemised (e.g. *she said he was a frigging lunatic*) or emasculated by the use of dots.

Little purpose is served by quoting mindless obscenities from the man in the street or, say, an athlete or soldier but you should consider using them if people prominent in public life use them in a context that gives their remarks great emphasis or throws in question their fitness to hold office.

You should draw to your editor's attention any story containing language that may be considered obscene or offensive.

obsolescent, obsolete   If something is *obsolescent* it is on the way to becoming *obsolete*.

OECD   Organisation for Economic Cooperation and Development (Paris). Established in 1961 to promote stable and sustainable economic growth in member countries and the expansion of world trade. Its 24 members in 1992 were the U.S., Canada, Japan, Australia, New Zealand, Turkey and all EC and EFTA (**q.v.**) members except Liechtenstein. Yugoslavia has associate status.

offensive language   See **obscenities**.

official titles   Be restrained in using idiomatic phrases to describe officials or official bodies rather than their official titles, e.g. *planning overlord, watchdog commission*. Such terms are often necessary in lead paragraphs where use of the full title would be clumsy, but the official title must be given in the body of the story. Avoid cliches and idioms with pejorative overtones like *trade union boss*.

officials   Do not describe government ministers as officials.

OIC   Organisation of the Islamic Conference, the principal world organisation of Moslem states, established in 1971, funded mainly by Saudi Arabia and based in Jeddah. Among OIC institutions is the Islamic Development Bank which provides soft loans for development projects in Islamic countries.

oil barrels   A barrel of oil is equivalent to 35 Imperial or 42 U.S. gallons or 159 litres. Convert barrels to metric tonnes by multiplying by 0.136, tonnes to barrels by multiplying by 7.33. One barrel per day (bpd) of crude oil production is equivalent to about 50 tonnes a year, depending on specific gravity.

To convert tonnes of oil precisely into barrels or kilolitres you need to know the specific gravity of the cargo. But you can get a rough conversion for crude cargoes from this list:

tonnes $\times$ 7.4 = bbl (barrels)

130,000 tonnes = 960,000 bbl
260,000 tonnes = 1.92 mln bbl = one VLCC products cargo
(which is a rough international standard)
tonnes × 1.2 = kl (kilolitres)

oil statistics   Oil production and export figures are usually expressed in terms of barrels per day (bpd) although they are sometimes quoted also in tonnes per year. To avoid confusing readers, standardise on bpd figures, normally giving them as a bracketed conversion after any figure expressed in tonnes per year. (See oil barrels for conversion ratios.)

Convert tonnes per year to barrels per day by dividing by 50.

As with all conversions, give an approximate conversion of an approximate figure and do not convert to more decimal places than are given in the original figure.

Also see **conversions, ton/tonnes**.

oil strikes   It is not correct to report the discovery of a new oil well. Nature does not provide ready-made oil wells awaiting discovery.

oil terms and definitions   These are some of the terms most often used in business stories about oil:

ADNOC prices – Official monthly selling prices of Abu Dhabi crude oil of Murban, Lower Zakum, Upper Zakum and Umm Shaif, issued retroactively by the state Abu Dhabi National Oil Co (ADNOC). Used as a benchmark in spot trading of Abu Dhabi crude, e.g. "December Murban traded at ADNOC plus 1.50 dlrs".

Allocations – Each seller looks at the nominations each has received for the month and allocates crude according to availability etc.

Asked – Refers to a seller's offering price.

Back-to-back – An arrangement in which a trader buys a cargo knowing that he has a specific buyer or outlet for it. The trader is acting as a middle man which gives him a margin of profit with very little financial risk.

Bid/offered – Buying and selling number respectively.

Broker – A broker in the international oil business is a person or company seeking to bring two parties together to close a piece of business. Usually the broker is paid by the seller.

Buy back oil – Where an original equity holder has given up (for recompense) to the government shareholding rights in a producing company. It sometimes retains, as part of the deal, the right to buy back some of the government's share.

C and **F** – Cost and Freight. The seller must pay the costs and freight necessary to bring the goods to the named destination, but the risk of loss or damage to the cargo is transferred from the seller to the buyer when the goods pass the ship's rail in the port of loading.

CIF – Cost, Insurance and Freight. It is the responsibility of the seller to arrange for the cargo of oil to be delivered and discharged at the port nominated by the buyer.

Confirmed – Indicates reporters have heard the names of both parties in a deal and have spoken to at least one of them for confirmation.

Delivered sale – Buyer takes risk and property in the goods only when they pass the vessel's permanent hose connection at the receiving installation.

Demurrage – The penalty paid by charterers or cargo suppliers/receivers for delaying a ship at a port of loading or discharge.

End-user – A company that buys or acquires hydrocarbons, either crude oil or products, for its own consumption and not for re-sale.

Equity oil – Oil obtained by an oil company by virtue of its shareholding in the producing company.

Feedstock – Hydrocarbons that can be used as the basic material fed into a refinery.

Five o'clocked – As in *Players had been five o'clocked* – in other words, they had been nominated Brent cargoes in the paper chain and run out of time to pass the cargo further down the chain, e.g.: *"There is a lot of five o'clock paranoia out there,"* said one trader.

FOB – Free on Board. The seller is responsible for placing on board the buyer's ship the goods as per contract. Risk of loss or damage to the goods is transferred from the seller to the buyer as the goods pass the ship's rails at port of loading.

GSP – Government selling price. The price that a producing government announces as its GSP. It will not necessarily actually sell at this price to anyone. Since producers started to sell their oil at prices linked to spot market quotations in discount competition in the late 1980s the GSPs have become a formality.

ICP – Indonesian crude price(s). Issued monthly by Indonesia's state oil company Pertamina.

Indicated – Refers to a seller's offering price.

MPM price – Official monthly selling price of Omani crude, notified retroactively by the Ministry of Petroleum and Mines (MPM) of Oman. Oman decides on the MPM after monitoring spot prices of its crude quoted by various energy services. Spot Oman cargoes trade at a premium or a discount to the MPM or at the MPM itself.

Nominations – Term contract holders submit nominations each month to the seller telling them how much crude they intend to lift that month.

OSP – Official selling price – same as GSP.

Print – The latest U.S. crude closing price of the corresponding traded month on the New York Mercantile Exchange. This number of the futures market is used for trading West Texas Intermediate (WTI) crude cargoes on the spot market, e.g. *December cash WTI traded at the print plus 10 cents a barrel in the Far East.*

Reported – Indicates reporters have heard the names of two parties involved in a deal but not spoken to either for confirmation.

Talked at – A general range within which buyers and sellers are discussing business.

Tender – A formal open request to submit offers to buy or sell, with the award being made to the most competitive offer. All bids have to be submitted by an agreed date and time and the winner should then be notified.

Term liftings – Oil lifted under a long-term contract agreement, as opposed to a spot purchase.

Trader – A company that buys and re-sells crude or product for profit.

Olympiad   Strictly this means the period of four years between two Olympic Games not the Games themselves.

on to   Two words.

ongoing   Usually tautological as in *the ongoing crisis*. If you need such a word use *continuing*.

only   As a rule *only* should go immediately before the word or phrase it qualifies. *Only SAS flies to the Faroes on Sunday* means that on a Sunday SAS is the only airline operating to the islands. *SAS flies only to the Faroes on Sunday* means that on Sunday the only SAS flight operating is to the islands. *SAS flies to the Faroes only on Sunday* means that the airline has only one flight a week to the islands.

OPEC   Organisation of Petroleum Exporting Countries (Vienna) founded in 1960. Its 13 members in 1992 were Algeria, Ecuador, Gabon, Indonesia, Iran, Iraq, Kuwait, Libya, Nigeria, Qatar, Saudi Arabia, United Arab Emirates and Venezuela. The acronym OPEC may be used at first reference if desired, preferably with a descriptive tag. Give the title in full at the second reference.

opera titles   House styles vary but it is usual to quote the title, whether italicised or not, and to capitalise every word in it apart from conjunctions, articles, particles and short prepositions, e.g. *"The Ring of the Nibelungen"*.

option   The right, acquired for a price, to buy a security (call option) or to sell it (put option) at an agreed price within a specified time.

options Not necessarily a synonym for *alternatives*. You can have only two alternatives but many options.

ordnance, ordinance *ordnance* is artillery, *ordinance* a decree.

orient Prefer *orientate*.

Oscars The statuettes presented annually by the Academy of Motion Picture Arts and Sciences. Also known as the Academy Awards.

others Beware of this word when reporting such things as accidents. It is usually unnecessary, as in *50 people were killed and 200 others injured.*

ounce To convert roughly to grams multiply by 30, precisely multiply by 28.35. Dry ounce = 28.35 grams, ounce troy = 31.10 grams. Liquid or fluid ounce – U.K. = 28.4 millilitres (20 fluid ounces = 1 pint) – U.S. = 29.6 millilitres (16 liquid ounces = 1 liquid pint).
See also **measures**.

ouster Except in a legal context the word is *ousting*. *Dismissal* or *overthrow* is better.

over *more than 100* is better than *over 100*.

overhead circuit A temporary dial-up or leased line, charged at a premium over a conventional leased circuit, dedicated to picture transmission.

overseas Do not write *overseas* when you mean *foreign*. France is not *overseas* from Germany but is *foreign* to Germany.

overused words See **journalese**.

Oxfam Oxford Committee for Famine Relief.

P

packet switching   A technique to make more efficient use of circuits by allowing a number of signals to be sent virtually simultaneously; this is achieved by assembling and then transmitting data in "packets", which also include addressing and sequence information. Several packets may be needed to complete a single message.

Pan-American   Hyphenated when referring to the two continents. But the now defunct airline was *Pan American World Airways* (*Pan American* or *Pan Am* for short).

Panchen Lama   See **Dalai Lama** and also **Tibet**.

paragraph   Each paragraph as a grammatical unit should deal with a single concept, whether in one, two or three sentences. If the ideas are disjointed use separate paragraphs for them. If you cannot deal with a single concept in a single paragraph of about three sentences, it is as well to start a new paragraph to give the reader a breathing space.

Vary paragraph length. A string of one-sentence paragraphs makes the story too staccato while a succession of lengthy paragraphs makes for indigestion. Two or at most three sentences is enough for most paragraphs. Lead paragraphs should run to no more than 30 words or so.

See also **leads, lead paragraphs**.

paraplegia   This is the total or partial paralysis of both legs while quadriplegia is the paralysis of all four limbs.

parliament   As a general rule refer to legislative assemblies initially as parliaments, irrespective of their formal names which can be given lower in the story, e.g. *Prime Minister John Major told Parliament . . . Replying to questions in the House of Commons, he said. . . .*

In the United States one can refer first either to *Congress* or, as appropriate, to *the Senate* or *the House of Representatives*. A member of the House may be described as a *representative* or as a *congressman/congresswoman*.

participate   Use *take part*.

participles   See **dangling participle**.

PC   Personal computer, a microprocessor-based computer used by a single individual.

pedal, peddle   You *pedal* a bicycle but *peddle* your wares.

peninsular   This is the adjective. The noun is *peninsula*.

p/e ratio   The price/earnings ratio is the current market price of a company's stock expressed as a multiple of its total per share earnings for the previous 12 months. The higher the p/e ratio the more a company's shares are being bought.

per cent   House styles vary but this is generally spelled as two words and not abbreviated.

Do not confuse percentage with percentage points. If a bank rate rises from one per cent to two per cent, it is a rise of one percentage point and an increase of 100 per cent not one per cent.

Note that a 100 per cent increase is twice the original figure, 200 per cent three times, 300 per cent four times, etc. It is a common error to write, for instance, that a 400 per cent rise means a quadrupling; in fact it means a fivefold increase.

To calculate percentages divide the first figure by the second and multiply by 100. For example 70 as a percentage of 350 is:

$$\frac{70 \times 100}{350} = 20 \text{ per cent}$$

Use a calculator for complicated figures and express the result to the nearest two decimal places, e.g. 75 expressed as a percentage of 350 is 21.42857142 or 21.43 per cent.

Always use decimals not fractions in percentages.

Persian Gulf   See **Gulf**.

persona non grata   A person, usually a diplomat or journalist, not acceptable in a certain country. Same spelling for men and women. Plural *personae non gratae*.

personal names   Use a given name and surname when first identifying people. Only if a given name is not available or if it is known that an individual prefers to be identified by his initials (e.g. *South African President F. W. de Klerk*) should you use initials.

See also **Chinese, Ethiopian, European, Hispanic, Korean, Portuguese, South African, Thai** and **Vietnamese names** and **capitalisation**.

persuade, convince   You *persuade* people to do something, *convince* them of something or that something is the case. Never write *convince to.* . . .

PGA   Professional Golfers' Association.

phenomenon   phenomena.

Philippines   The Philippines faces two insurgent movements. The Communist New People's Army (NPA) has been fighting since 1969 to establish a Marxist state. Its strength was estimated at about 18,500 in 1991. The Moro National Liberation Front (MNLF) launched a revolt in 1972 to demand independence for the southern island of Mindanao, ancestral home of the country's estimated five million Moslem minority. Although a ceasefire was signed in 1986 sporadic guerrilla incidents have continued.

See also **Filipino**.

phoney   Not *phony*.

phosphorus   Not *phosphorous*.

picture captions   See **captions**.

pilots   Military aircraft other than strategic bombers and transports normally carry only one pilot. Write *the two crew* not *the two pilots* when reporting incidents involving fighter-bombers and the like.

pistol   See **weapons**.

play titles   House styles vary but generally titles of non-English plays and films should be given in the original language as well as English, with the version that is better known internationally mentioned first. They should be in quotation marks, whether italicised or not, e.g. *"Les Liaisons Dangereuses" (Dangerous Liaisons)*. Capitalise every word in the title apart from conjunctions, articles, particles and short prepositions, e.g. *"The Merchant of Venice"*.

PLO   Palestine (not Palestinian) Liberation Organisation.

plural forms   See **nouns**.

plurality This word is used, especially in the United States, to mean a winning vote short of 50 per cent in contrast to a majority, which means more than 50 per cent.

p.m. Time: post meridiem (after noon) e.g. *3 p.m.*

poems House styles vary but generally quote the title, whether italicised or not, and capitalise every word in it apart from conjunctions, articles, particles and short prepositions, e.g. *"The Lay of the Last Minstrel"*.

pointed out Avoid this term if the statement is in any way contentious since it suggests that you accept that what the speaker is *saying is a fact. Said* is better.

political parties Capitalise the names of political parties and of movements with a specific doctrine, e.g. *a Communist official, a Democratic senator.* Use lower case for non-specific references, e.g. *The settlement was run on communist principles. He proposed a democratic vote.*

Polynesia See **Melanesia**.

pool copy Ground rules for pools should be clearly defined in advance. Basically there are two kinds of pools – those in which a single story is written on behalf of all pool members and those in which individual pool members write their own stories which are filed on a collective pool basis. If you know that a journalist from your organisation has written the story you may use his or her byline.

   If another correspondent has written the pooled report a byline should not be used unless it says for whom the writer works.

Portuguese names Like the Spanish, Portuguese and Brazilians include the family names of both their father and their mother in their full names. Unlike the Spanish, they put the mother's name before the father's and they normally retain both names at second reference. Where they use one it would always be the patronymic, i.e. the last name. Thus *Jose Cabral Nettim* could be either *Cabral Nettim* or *Nettim* at second reference.

posh Slang. Avoid.

pound Abbreviation *lb* (no full stop, same singular and plural) acceptable at all references. To convert roughly to grams multiply by 900 and divide by 2, precisely multiply by 454. To convert roughly to kilograms multiply by 9 and divide by 20, precisely multiply by 0.454. See also **measures**.

pour, pore   You *pour* a liquid and *pore* over maps and documents.

practicable, practical   Something *practicable* is something that can be done. Something *practical* is useful.

practice, practise   *practice* is the noun, *practise* the verb.

pre-   If the second element of a word beginning with *pre-* starts with an *e*, hyphenate, e.g. *pre-empt*.

precondition   Tautological. *Condition* is enough.

premier   As a general rule use *premier* for the heads of government of states that are part of a larger political entity, e.g. the Australian and German states and the Canadian provinces. Reserve *prime minister* for the heads of government of sovereign states, although *premier* may be used for brevity in a headline.

pre-planned   Tautological. *Planned* is enough.

pre-press system   A computer system dedicated to page layout for newspapers or magazines. It also handles colour printing.

prescribe, proscribe   *prescribe* is to set down as an order, *proscribe* to prohibit.

presently   Use to mean *in a short time* or *soon* – not, as in American usage, *at present*. In the latter sense *currently* is the word you want.

press conference   Use *news conference* unless the electronic media have been excluded.

press reports   When picking up newspaper, radio or television reports, name your source. Do not refer just to *press reports*.
    The fact that you are quoting a news report does not exonerate you from responsibility for providing a file that is accurate, balanced and not defamatory. You should not pick up without careful checking reports that seem improbable or irresponsible.
    You should help your readers or listeners assess the likely accuracy of reports picked up in this way by inserting relevant background and by giving some indication of the political stance, reliability and potential for bias of the source quoted.
    Such phrases as *state-run radio, left-wing newspaper, mass-circulation*

tabloid, columnist usually well informed on defence matters or *Communist Party daily* enable readers to make their own judgment of the likely truth of the report.

pressurise   Use *press* or *pressure* unless speaking of industrial processes.

prestigious   Avoid this pompous and often tautological word. If something is prestigious, or famous, then you need hardly say so.

prime minister   Capitalise when referring, for example, to *Prime Minister John Major*. Use lower case when referring simply to *the prime minister*.

prime rate   In the United States prime rate is a benchmark reference for determining interest rates on short-term loans to high-quality large borrowers. The actual rate could be lower but more often it is higher than the benchmark. Sometimes used erroneously to imply it is the bank's lowest rate.

Revolving home equity loans and some small-business loans are still tied to the U.S. prime rate but corporate loans and mortgages are more and more often being linked to indices set by the markets, like certificates of deposit or Treasury bill rates.

principal, principle   *principle* is always a noun, meaning a fundamental basis or truth. *principal* can be an adjective, meaning chief, or a noun meaning chief person, as in *principal of a school*, or capital sum, as in *debt principal*.

prior to   Prefer *before*.

Procter and Gamble　Not *Proctor and Gamble.*

profanity　See **obscenities**.

proforma　A pre-set page in an editing system designed for regular items of text or figures. Only the variable information needs to be keyed in, thus speeding input.

program　Use this spelling only in stories about computers and for stock market program trading. Otherwise *programme.*

pronouns　There must never be any doubt about the noun to which a pronoun refers. In *The president told the prime minister he was the target of an assassination plot* it is unclear whether the president or the prime minister is the target. Recast such sentences to eliminate the ambiguity.

Who is the subject, *whom* the object of a verb. As a rough guide as to which word to use, substitute *he* or *him* for the *who* or *whom* and see which makes sense.

Examples: *Brown, whom the prosecution says planned the robbery, is. . . .* Would you say *Him planned the robbery?* No. So the correct word is *who.*

Brown, who the prosecution accused of planning the robbery, is. . . . Would you say *The prosecution accused he?* No. So the correct word is *whom.*

But be guided by common usage and be ready to use *who* as the object if this sounds more natural, e.g. *Who she met at the midnight rendezvous is not yet known.*

You and I is almost invariably wrong. *You* and *I*, as nominatives, must be the subject of the sentence and you would normally use *we* unless you wrote for emphasis, e.g. *You and I will never agree.* In 19 cases out of 20 if not 99 out of 100 the correct form is *you and me*, e.g. *The case against you and me will be heard next week.*

Avoid the clumsy *he or she* usage by switching to the plural, e.g. not *If a journalist crosses the police line he or she is likely to be arrested* but *If journalists cross the police line they are likely to be arrested.*

Use neuter pronouns for countries, ships, cars, aircraft, animals, etc., e.g. *Portugal and its territories, aboard the liner when it sailed.* The occasional bright story may be enhanced by the use of a feminine or masculine pronoun to personalise a machine or animal, but these should be rare exceptions.

propeller　Not *propellor.*

proscribe, prescribe *proscribe* is to prohibit, *prescribe* to set down as an order.

protagonist The leading actor in a drama. *A leading protagonist* is tautological. Strictly speaking a drama may have only one protagonist. The word is a current favourite of journalists who think long words enhance their copy. Phrases such as *chief figure* or *rival leaders* are better.

protest You *protest* your innocence, *protest against* your conviction.

protester Not *protestor*.

proven Use *proved* except in two cases: in writing of oil reserves or of the Scottish legal verdict *not proven* (neither guilty nor not guilty).

PTT Generically, any organisation that runs a national communications service (originally post, telegraph and telephone).

punctuation These are some points that regularly cause problems.

adjectives (hyphenation): When using an adjective and a noun together as an adjective, hyphenate them, e.g. *a blue-chip share, high-caste Hindus*. When using an adjective and the past participle of a verb together adjectivally, hyphenate them, e.g. *old-fashioned morality, rose-tinted spectacles*.

adverbs (hyphenation): When using an adverb and an adjective together adjectivally do not hyphenate them, e.g. *a perfectly clear sky* not *a perfectly-clear sky*.
    When using an adverb and the past participle of a verb together adjectivally, hyphenate them, e.g. *an ill-considered plan, a well-known singer*.

apostrophes: Use the apostrophe according to the following rules, unless to do so would lead to a word that looked or sounded very strange.
    Singular words and plural words not ending in *s* form the possessive by adding *'s*, e.g. *Boeing's new airliner, the children's books*. Plural words already ending in *s* form the possessive by adding the apostrophe alone, e.g. *the soldiers' weapons*.
    There is usually no problem about using the apostrophe with words ending in *s*. *the class's performance, the princess's return, Schultz's car* are all acceptable because they can be pronounced easily. Some words would look or sound so odd, e.g. *the Dukakises' son, Jesus's sermons* or *Tunis's main prison*, that it is best to write your way out of trouble. Recast such phrases, e.g. *the son of the Dukakises, the sermons of Jesus* or *the main prison in Tunis*.
    Note that *it's* is an abbreviation of *it is*. The possessive form of the pronoun *it* is *its*.

Do not use an apostrophe in words like *the 1990s* or abbreviations like *NCOs*.

colons: Use a colon before directly quoting a complete sentence and as a signal that you are about to list things advertised in the preceding words, e.g. *. . . these were: three French hens, two turtle doves and a partridge in a pear tree.*

Put the word following a colon in lower case unless the next word is a proper name, a direct quotation or the beginning of a sentence.

commas: Do not over-punctuate, especially with commas. Any sentence studded with commas could probably benefit from a rewrite.

Use commas as a guide to sense, to break a sentence into logically discrete parts, but do not use them to the extent that they break the flow of a sentence.

Use commas to mark off words and phrases that are in apposition to or define other words or phrases in the sentence e.g. *Roland Dumas, French foreign minister, said . . . Rudolf Nureyev, most prominent of the defectors from the Bolshoi, has danced. . . .*

Use commas to mark off a clause that is not essential to the meaning of a sentence, e.g. *The airliner, which was seven years old, crashed. . . .* But a clause that cannot be removed from the sentence without affecting its meaning is not marked off by commas, e.g. *The airliner that crashed on Thursday was seven years old whereas the plane lost the previous day was brand new.*

Use commas to separate items in a list, e.g. *cheese, fruit, wine and coffee* or *Smith despised ballet, hated the theatre and was bored by opera.* Note that there is normally no comma before the final *and*. However, a comma should be used in this position if to leave it out would risk ambiguity, e.g. *He admired Irving Berlin, Rodgers and Hart, and Leonard Bernstein.*

As in the sentence above, a comma follows an initial *however*. But as long as there is no risk of ambiguity there is no need for the comma after opening phrases like *On Wednesday the committee decided . . . In the first four months of 1992 Poland exported. . . .*

A comma is often needed before *and* or *but* in the middle of a compound sentence to make clear where the new clause begins. *They gave the prize to Jones and his wife, and the family was delighted* is very different from *They gave the prize to Jones, and his wife and family were delighted.* Delete the comma and the result is complete ambiguity. But no comma is needed when both or all parts of a compound sentence have the same subject, e.g. *They gave the first prize to Jones and the second prize to his wife.*

Commas, semi-colons and full stops go outside closing brackets and closing quotes if the quote forms less than a complete sentence. If the quote forms a complete sentence the comma, etc., goes before the closing quote.

dashes: Use dashes sparingly to enclose parenthetical matter, e.g. *Finally -- indeed with only minutes to go before the deadline -- the government backed down.* Never use dashes to set off relative clauses in a sentence.

For the sake of clarity, dashes should be double (--) and hyphens single (-).

Dashes are followed by lower case unless they are used to label sections of a list, e.g.

The study concluded:
-- Almost half had more exports this year than last.
-- In 1990 a third had less imports than in 1989.
-- One in five expects better terms of trade in 1991.

exclamation mark: This is grossly overused, particularly by tabloid newspapers, to inject spurious drama. A safe rule would be to use it in text or headlines only when it is a legitimate part of a quotation.

hyphenation: Usage varies wildly and there are few clear rules. In general, when in doubt leave it out. But use the hyphen if its omission might lead to ambiguity, e.g. *three year-old horses* is quite different from *three-year-old horses*. Hyphens tend to erode with time, and many words once hyphenated are now generally written unhyphenated, e.g. *ceasefire, cooperation, gunrunner, machinegun.*

Use a hyphen to show that two or more words are to be read together as a single word with its own meaning, different from that of the individual words, e.g. *extra-judicial duties* (duties other than judicial ones) as opposed to *extra judicial duties* (additional judicial duties).

When using an adjective and a noun together as an adjective, hyphenate them, e.g. *a blue-chip share, high-caste Hindus.* When using an adjective and the past participle of a verb together adjectivally, hyphenate them, e.g. *old-fashioned morality, rose-tinted spectacles.*

Do not hyphenate an adjective and a noun when they stand alone, e.g. *the left wing of the party.* If the adjective and noun are paired to form a new adjective, they are hyphenated, e.g. *a first-class result, the left-wing party.* Hyphenate numbers and nouns or adjectives when they are paired to form a new adjective, e.g. *a six-cylinder car, a one-armed man.*

Do not hyphenate an adverb and adjective when they stand alone, e.g. *The artist was well known.* If the adverb and adjective are paired to form a new adjective, they are hyphenated, e.g. *a well-known artist.* Do not do so however if the adverb ends in *-ly*, e.g. *a poorly planned operation.*

Hyphenate two adjectives or an adjective and a present or past participle when they are paired to form a new adjective, e.g. a *dark-blue dress, a good-looking man, a well-tailored suit.*

If the second element in a word is capitalised, hyphenate, e.g. *anti-Semitism* (although *transatlantic* is widely accepted). If *pre-* or *re-* is followed by an element beginning with *e*, hyphenate, e.g. *pre-empt, re-employ.*

If the first element of a word is the negative *non-*, hyphenate, e.g. *a non-aggression pact* (but *nonconformist*).

Where two nouns are paired to form another noun, hyphenate if their original distinct meanings are still clearly retained, e.g. *actor-manager*. Otherwise do not hyphenate, e.g. *housekeeper*.

Where a verb and adverb are paired to form a noun, hyphenate if the verb ends and the adverb begins with a vowel, e.g. *cave-in, flare-up*.

Hyphenate titles when the first word is a preposition, e.g. *under-secretary, vice-admiral*, or when a noun is followed by an adjective, e.g. *attorney-general*. Do not hyphenate when the noun follows the adjective, e.g. *second lieutenant*.

Hyphenate fractions, e.g. *three-quarters, two-thirds*.

Hyphenate secondary compass points, e.g. *south-southwest*, but not main ones, e.g. *southwest*.

Hyphenate compound words when not to do so would result in an ugly sound or confusion of meaning, e.g. *cross-section, sea-eagle*.

Hyphenate both terms in phrases such as *short- and medium-range missiles*. If a figure being converted is hyphenated make sure that the figure in the conversion is also, e.g. *within a 10-mile (six-km) radius*.

quotation marks: Whether you use single or double quote marks be sure that you are consistent, closing the quote with the same mark as you used to open it. If you use double quotes, then use single quotes for a subordinate quotation within the main passage and vice versa, e.g. *He said: "No one whose motto is 'Give me liberty or give me death' will be turned away."* Precede a full sentence in quotes by a colon. A final full stop or question mark goes within the quotes when it ends a complete sentence, outside the quotes when it ends only part of a sentence, e.g. *I have no sympathy with those who cry "Home Rule for Wales"*.

See also **Arab names, compass points, slugs**.

Punjab   Sikh militants are fighting for an independent homeland they call Khalistan (Land of the Pure) in the rich agricultural north Indian state of Punjab. Thousands of people have been killed in a decade-old campaign which intensified in 1984 when then Prime Minister Indira Gandhi sent the army into Amritsar's Golden Temple against separatists using it as their headquarters. More than 1,000 people were killed and four months later Gandhi was assassinated by her Sikh bodyguards in revenge for what most Sikhs saw as an appalling act of sacrilege. Punjab was placed under direct rule from Delhi in January 1987. Sikh politicians accuse Indian security forces of torture and organising extra-judicial murders through vigilante groups.

purchase   *buy* is shorter, better.

pyramid construction   Also known as *inverted pyramid construction*, this method of writing arranges information in descending order of significance and interest. A story can then be cut from the bottom upwards, always leaving a self-contained version.

Q

QE2 The only acceptable abbreviation for the Cunard liner Queen Elizabeth 2. It may be used at first reference.

quadriplegia This is the paralysis of all four limbs as opposed to paraplegia which is the total or partial paralysis of both legs.

quantum leap A sudden and spectacular advance.

Quebec Largest of Canada's 10 provinces, Quebec has a population of 6.5 million, 85 per cent of them descended from French colonists. Quebec voters in 1976 elected the separatist Parti Quebecois but later rejected its proposal to negotiate sovereignty from Canada in 1980. Polls in 1990 showed two-thirds of Quebec voters supported sovereignty-association, vaguely defined as a politically independent Quebec having an economic association with Canada, while more than half favoured outright independence. The province's Liberal Party, in power since 1985, advocates a renewed federalism giving Quebec greater autonomy.

queen *Queen Elizabeth* at first reference and *the queen* or *Queen Elizabeth* at second reference, although in British and Commonwealth newspaper house styles it is more usual to make *Queen* upper case at all references. In Britain write *Queen Elizabeth the Queen Mother* at first reference if she is the subject of the story. If she is listed simply among other members of the royal family use the short form *the Queen Mother*. This is capitalised at all references.

quip "The president/prime minister/prince quipped . . ." is a phrase almost invariably followed by something that is not funny. Avoid both *quip* and third-rate humour, however eminent the quipster.

Quoran Use *Koran*.

quotation Quotes personalise stories and give them immediacy. Try to get a quote into the first three paragraphs of any story where it is appropriate.

Selective use of quotes can be unbalanced. Be sure that quotes you use are representative of what the speaker is saying and that you describe body language (a smile or a wink) that may affect the sense of what is being reported.

Avoid unnecessary broken quotes (**q.v.**) and do not use them in a lead paragraph unless the words have special significance or relevance. Any such partial quote must be backed up with a full quote later in the story.

Quotes are sacred. Do not alter anything put in quotation marks other than to delete words, and then only if the deletion does not alter the sense of the quote. You should delete routine obscenities (**q.v.**).

Show deletions from a quoted text with three (or, depending on house style, four) full stops closed up, e.g. *He said: "We will win by fair means or foul . . . and the devil take the hindmost."*

If you need to background or explain a quote do so in a separate paragraph or by bracketing a phrase into the quoted remarks, e.g. *He said: "They (the Khmer Rouge) are bound to fail."*

Where you are quoting the same source for a lengthy statement you need not repeat the source paragraph by paragraph as long as there is no doubt who is speaking.

Avoid quotes in colloquial or parochial language not easily translated or understood in other countries. If you do give such quotes, explain what they mean, e.g. *He said: "Bush is behind the eight ball (in a difficult situation)."*

When translating quotes from another language into your own you should normally do so in an idiomatic way rather than with pedantic literalness. However, if a statement is tendentious and likely to be the subject of close analysis give a literal translation.

If an entire sentence is in quotation marks, put the full stop before the closing quote, e.g. *He said: "We will win by fair means or foul."* If the quoted passage, however long, does not constitute a full sentence, put the full stop after the closing quote, e.g. *He said they would win "by fair means or foul".*

Do not end one paragraph with a close quote and begin the next with an open quote. If the quote is continuous, the close quote is not needed. If the quotes are not consecutive, then end the paragraph with three full stops (e.g. *. . . and we will never surrender . . .*) or begin the second paragraph with, e.g. *He also said . . .* or *She added . . .*

A statement that follows a colon quote begins with a capital, e.g.

Guzhenko said: "The conference ignored the principle of equality."

House styles vary but normally you quote the titles of films, plays and books but not of ships, aircraft, newspapers or magazines.

See also **broken quotes, deletion**.

R

race Mention a person's race, colour or ethnic or religious affiliation only if it is relevant to the story.

If race is relevant, *black*, *white* and *of mixed race* are acceptable adjectives. Avoid words like *African*, *Asian* or *European* unless an individual's nationality is not known.

Use the term *coloured* only for South Africans of mixed race.

Do not use *Negro* as an indicator of racial origin unless making a special historical or similar point.

rack, wrack Use *wrack* only for seaweed and in the phrase *wrack and ruin*. Otherwise use *rack*.

Ramadan The month of fasting when devout Moslems refrain from all food, drink or sex during daylight hours and focus on devotion and good works. The majority Sunnis fast between dawn and sunset, the Shia from dawn to dusk. The start and end of the month for most Islamic countries depends on the sighting of the new moon by the naked eye. It is the ninth and holiest month of the Islamic, lunar calendar.

re- If the second element of a word beginning with *re-* starts with an *e*, hyphenate, e.g. *re-employ*.

reassure Use this word with caution. It means *to give a new assurance*. It does not mean that the person to whom the assurance is given is necessarily reassured. (e.g. *Hitler reassured Czechoslovakia that he had no designs on its territory*). Better to write *again assured*.

rebut Use with care. It means *to refute* not just *to argue against* so its use implies an editorial judgment.

record Do not write *He set a new world record*. By definition any record that has just been set is new.

recourse, resource, resort You may have *recourse* to your newspaper's library to establish a company's *resources*. As a last *resort* you may have to consult stock exchange records.

Red Cross   The Red Cross movement comprises the International Committee of the Red Cross (ICRC); the League of Red Cross and Red Crescent Societies; and national societies around the world. Both the ICRC (founded in 1863 and composed exclusively of Swiss citizens) and the league (1919) are based in Geneva. The ICRC helps victims of war and internal conflicts. The league brings relief to victims of natural disasters and helps care for refugees outside areas of conflict.

The ICRC's work in protecting wounded and sick servicemen, prisoners of war and civilians in times of armed conflict is based upon international humanitarian law enshrined in the four Geneva conventions of 1949 and two additional protocols signed in 1977.

Give the ICRC title in full at first reference; do not abbreviate to the *International Red Cross*. For the sake of brevity in a lead paragraph you can refer to *a Red Cross official* or spokesman as long as you make clear lower in the story that he belongs to the ICRC.

referendum   *referenda*.

refinancing   See **loans**.

refute   This means *to disprove* not *to deny* or *reject*. Avoid it except in a direct quote.

regime   A word with negative overtones in political context. Use *government*.

religions   Names of divinities are capitalised but unspecific plurals are lower case, e.g. *Allah, the Almighty, Christ, God, Jehovah, the Deity, the Holy Trinity, Zeus* but *the gods, the lords of the universe*.

Capitalise names of denominations and religious movements, e.g. *Baptist, Buddhist, Christian, Church of England, the Church (meaning the body of believers), Islamic, Moslem, Orthodox*. But non-denominational references are lower case, e.g. *adult baptism, orthodox beliefs, churches (meaning the buildings), built a temple*.

religious titles   Capitalise when they accompany a personal name, otherwise use lower case, e.g. *Bishop Thaddeus Smith, Dean Robert Jones*, but *the bishop, the dean*. Use only the simplest and best-known titles at first reference, e.g. *the Rev. Jesse Jackson, Dr John Smith* rather than *the Right Rev. John Smith*.

Renamo   Acronym for Mozambican National Resistance. Do not abbreviate to *MNR*.

renegue Use *renege*.

repechage In sport, a contest between runners-up.

repetition Avoid excessive repetition of words and of stereotyped descriptions of people or things, but do not overdo the search for variations.

If you are writing about Thailand call it *Thailand* and not *the Southeast Asian country*. It is better to repeat *the United Nations* than to avoid repetition by calling it *the world body*.

reported, reportedly If you use the word *reported* without stating the source at once, you must give it in the next sentence or paragraph. Do not use *reportedly*.

reported speech Do not retain the present indicative in reported speech. Change *is* to *was*, *are* to *were*, *will* and *shall* to *would*, *has* and *have* to *had*. Thus it is: "He said it was . . ." not "He said it is . . ."

There is an exception in the case of lead paragraphs with the source at the end instead of the beginning of the sentence, where to avoid the present indicative would lead to lack of clarity or smack of pedantry.

For example, it is acceptable to write in a lead paragraph: *Mobiloil will order three new supertankers from the Pusan shipyard in Korea next month, the company said.* If the source were at the beginning, we would write: *Mobiloil said it would order three new supertankers from the Pusan shipyard. . . .*

It is usually unnecessary to follow *said* with *that*.

repudiation See **loans**.

requirements *needs* is shorter, better.

rescheduling See **loans**.

restaurateur One who runs a restaurant. Not *restauranteur*.

restructuring See **loans**.

revaluation See **currency**.

reveal Use with caution. Use of the word implies (a) that you accept that the statement is true and (b) that the information had previously been kept secret, which may not be the case.

reverend Abbreviated to *Rev.* Write *the Rev. John Smith* not *Rev. John Smith*.

revolver   See **weapons**.

rial, riyal   The *rial* is the currency of Iran and Oman, the *riyal* that of Qatar and Saudi Arabia. See **Middle Eastern currencies**.

Richter scale   See **earthquakes**.

right wing   *a right-winger, a right-wing politician*, but *the right wing* of the political spectrum.

rocks   Americans throw **rocks**. Elsewhere people throw *stones*.

Rolls-Royce   Note hyphen.

Roman Catholic Church   Pope John Paul II is head of the Church, which has about 850 million members. The former Cardinal Karol Wojtyla of Krakow, Poland, was elected on October 16, 1978, as first non-Italian Pontiff in 455 years. The Pope holds numerous titles, including Vicar of Jesus Christ, Primate of the West and Primate of Italy, which are not normally used. He is the head of Vatican City, a 108-acre (44-hectare) sovereign state in Rome. At first reference *Pope John Paul*, at subsequent references *the Pope* or *the Pontiff* or *John Paul*. The Pope's closest advisers are known as cardinals, who are appointed by him. Those under 80 can enter a conclave to elect a new Pope. At first reference *Cardinal John Doe*. At subsequent references *the cardinal* or *Doe*. A high-ranking member of the Church, such as a cardinal, an archbishop or a bishop can be referred to subsequently as a prelate. Monsignor is someone who has a rank between priest and bishop, e.g. *Monsignor Martin Smith*. In some countries, such as Italy, France and Spain and in Latin America, monsignor is a catchall title used for monsignors, bishops, archbishops and cardinals, e.g. *the Archbishop of Bogota, Monsignor Enrique Perez*. Avoid this usage. Use *Boston Archbishop Charles Dust*. For priests, use *Father John Doe*. Do not use *the Rev., Reverend* or *Most Reverend*.

The Church hierarchy goes like this: priest, monsignor, bishop, archbishop, cardinal, Pope. The Church government working in the Vatican is known as the Curia. The Vatican technically refers to the city-state in Rome and the Holy See to the Church's central administration, but the terms have become interchangeable in common use. The Holy See's ambassadors around the world are known as *papal nuncios* and its embassies as *nunciatures*.

In some countries, such as Poland and Hungary, the highest-ranking Church official has the title *primate* for historical reasons. At first reference *the Primate of Poland, Cardinal Jozef Glemp*; but *the head of Poland's Roman Catholic Church, Cardinal Jozef Glemp*, is better. The Pope is also head of Eastern Catholic Churches in communion with Rome. They worship in a different rite and have their own patriarchs or primates. Some of them allow married men to become priests.

Romania   Not *Rumania*.

RORO   roll on/roll off vehicle ferry.

Rosh Hashanah   The Jewish New Year festival.

round figures   Figures are normally rounded to two significant decimals, with halves rounded upwards. Thus *15.564* becomes *15.56*, while *15.565* becomes *15.57*. See **figures**.

royalty   House styles vary but normally one retains the titles of rulers and their consorts at second reference, e.g. *King Hussein, Queen Beatrix, Sheikh Isa or the king, the queen, the sheikh*. The titles of other members of royal families can be dropped at second reference.

In Britain, for instance, Queen Elizabeth's husband is *the Duke of Edinburgh*, at second reference *the duke* or *Prince Philip*. Her eldest son is *Prince Charles, Prince of Wales*. Either title can be used at first reference; then *Charles* or *the prince*. His wife is formally *the Princess of Wales* and can be so called at first reference although the title *Princess Diana*, which is technically not correct, may also be used. At subsequent references simply *Diana*. When she is the subject of the story refer to *Queen Elizabeth the Queen Mother* by her full title at first reference. At second reference, or at first reference if she is only mentioned in passing, *the Queen Mother*.

Use Roman numerals in referring to royalty, e.g. *Charles I, Louis XIV* not *Charles the First, Louis the Fourteenth*.

Ruanda Use *Rwanda*, Central Africa.

ruble Use *rouble*.

Rumania Use *Romania*.

rumours Rumours, including unconfirmed press reports and trade speculation, can particularly affect the international money, stock and commodity markets and create a difficult reporting situation. If you are an economic journalist you identify what item of rumour or gossip is having a market impact, check it as thoroughly as possible and report it responsibly. It is prudent to report only rumours that have a material market impact and to show that every effort has been made to have them confirmed or denied.

Follow these guidelines:

Treat all rumours with caution. Try to pinpoint their origin.

Report them only if they are having a significant market impact.

Seek fast confirmation/denial from appropriate, authoritative sources. It is wise to include this comment in the lead of your story, even if the best you can get is *no comment* or *A spokesman was not available for comment.*

Do not give up when confirmation/denial is not immediately available. Get official comment as quickly as possible.

Do not just say how a price is affected by a rumour. Always add why the market views it as bullish or bearish.

When rumours continue to affect markets, always include at each reference to them whatever official reaction there is.

If one source tells you a rumour, do not call other sources and quote them the same report. Just ask how they account for the price change.

Do not write of *unconfirmed rumours.* A rumour by definition is unconfirmed.

In trying to check unofficial reports of the death or serious illness of major political figures you must not lay yourself open to a charge of spreading irresponsible rumours.

See also **hoaxes, sourcing**.

Russia(n) See **Soviet** entries.

Russian names Use *-sky* not *-ski* at the end of Russian names, e.g. *Petrovsky* not *Petrovski*.

S

SAC   Strategic Air Command (U.S.).

Sahel   A belt of countries spanning sub-Saharan Africa, prone to repeated drought and famine. Definitions of the Sahel vary but Reuters regards it as comprising Burkina Faso, Cape Verde, Chad, Gambia, Guinea-Bissau, Mali, Mauritania, Niger, Senegal and Sudan.

Saigon   Now *Ho Chi Minh City*, Vietnam.

Sahrawi   The people of the Western Saharan republic proclaimed by Polisario guerrillas fighting for independence from Morocco. Its full name is the *Saharan Arab Democratic Republic*.

SALT   Strategic Arms Limitation Talks. U.S.-Soviet negotiations which led to the 1972 SALT-1 treaty, freezing the number of the superpowers' ballistic missile launchers at existing levels. Further talks produced the 1979 SALT-2 treaty, which sought to limit multiple-warhead missiles. Succeeded in 1982 by the Strategic Arms Reduction Talks (START) (**q.v.**).

Salvadorean   Not *Salvadoran*.

SAM   surface-to-air missile.

sanction   Avoid *sanction* as a verb. It has conflicting meanings, *to approve* and *to punish*.

Sandinista   Not *Sandinist*. The Sandinista left-wing guerrillas seized power in a coup in Nicaragua in 1979 but were defeated in elections in 1990. See also **Contra**.

Saudi Aramco   *Aramco* is the acronym for *Arabian American Oil Company*, now wholly owned by the Saudi government.

Scandinavia   This comprises Denmark, Norway and Sweden. The Nordic countries are these three plus Finland and Iceland. Because of the danger of confusion list the countries even if you use Nordic or Scandinavian in a lead for the sake of brevity.

scanner   A device that scans a picture and transfers it to an adjacent storage device for manipulation or onward transmission.

scrip issue   An extra issue of shares to existing shareholders, who do not have to pay for them.

SEAQ   The computerised London Stock Exchange Automated Quotations system which constantly logs share prices.

seasons   Be careful in writing of summer and winter, spring and autumn, since the seasons are reversed north and south of the equator. Do not impose northern norms upon the south.

second lieutenant   Two words.

Second World War   Or *World War Two*. Not *WWII*.

Security Council   The U.N. Security Council becomes *the council* (lower case) at second reference.

seize   Not *sieze*.

sentence length   Sentences should generally be short but, to avoid a staccato effect, vary their length. Avoid complex constructions. A sentence with more than two subordinate clauses can be hard to follow. A sentence whose grammatical structure is complicated or sounds pompous usually benefits by being rewritten or even divided into two.

separate   Not *seperate*.

Sephardim   Jews of Spanish or Portuguese descent as opposed to Ashkenazim who are Jews of East or Central European descent. Adjectives *Sephardic, Ashkenazic*.

Sevastopol   Not *Sebastopol*, Crimea.

sexist language   The media should not use language that perpetuates the stereotype of women as the weaker, inferior sex. Such language is offensive, out of date and often simply inaccurate. Sexist references should be avoided, as should such linguistic absurdities as creating the crime of *peopleslaughter*.

It is wrong to assume that police, firefighters or soldiers are always men. *Police* is shorter than *policemen* anyway. Most armies can be said to deploy *troops* or *soldiers* rather than *men*, avoiding any need to worry about whether women are among them.

To say *police set up roadblocks* is more active than saying *manned*.

Man doesn't explore space alone any more. People do, and they can *crew* a ship or *staff* an office.

Do not identify a woman as such unless her gender is pertinent to the story. Where possible use the same term for men and women, e.g. *mayor* or *poet*, not *mayoress* or *poetess*. There are some well-established exceptions like *actor, actress*. But use *chairman, chairwoman* not *chair*.

Avoid the *he or she* problem by using the plural. Write *Astronauts must be fit. They . . .* not *An astronaut must be fit. He or she. . . .*

The fact that Margaret Thatcher is a woman and a grandmother is no more relevant to most stories that the fact that George Bush is a man and a grandfather. Do not describe her dress or hairstyle where you would not describe his.

While stories about women breaking into fields of work traditionally monopolised by men are legitimate, never use language that suggests there is something remarkable about a woman doing what in the past has been considered a man's job, e.g. *Maryann Smith may be only five foot two and weigh 96 pounds but the snub-nosed blonde can hew 20 tons of coal a day. . . .*

Use *woman* not *lady*. Any female over 18 is a *woman* not a *girl*.

SHAPE Supreme Headquarters Allied Powers Europe. Based in Mons, Belgium, it is the military headquarters of NATO and works closely with the political headquarters in Brussels.

sheikh An Arab chief. Not *shaikh*. Use title and name at all references, e.g. *Sheikh Isa*. Do not write *the sheikh*.

Shia Also *Shi'ite*. See **Sunni**.

ship tonnage See **tonnage of ships**.

ship types and sizes These are the main types and sizes of oil tankers and bulk carriers:

Tankers   Ultra large crude carriers (ULCCS) – 300,000 dwt or over
    Very large crude carriers (VLCCs) – 200,000–300,000 dwt
    Suezmax – 140,000 dwt
    Aframax – 79,999 dwt

Bulkers (bulk carriers)
    Very large bulk carriers (VLBCs) – 200,000 dwt
    Cape-sized – 100,000 to 150,000 dwt
    Panamax-sized – 70,000 dwt, maximum width 32 metres
    Handy-sized – 25,000 to 45,000 dwt.

ships' names   Do not use *HMS* or *USS* to designate British or American warships if the nationality of the ship is already clear. Write *the British frigate Battleaxe* not *the British frigate HMS Battleaxe*. But in datelines write, for instance, *ABOARD HMS BATTLEAXE*.

Routinely check the names of ships in Jane's Fighting Ships, Lloyd's Register or the weekly Lloyd's Shipping Index. Do not put quotation marks round the names of ships. Always use neuter pronouns.

siege   Not *seige*.

simplex   Describes a circuit that can carry traffic in only one direction, without error correction.

single out   By definition, this phrase should be used only for single examples. Do not write, for instance, *He singled out Britain, France and Italy for blame*.

Sinhalese   The major ethnic group in Sri Lanka.

sjambok   A South African whip, sometimes used by police.

skipper   Use only of fishing vessels. Otherwise *captain*.

slang   Avoid slang that may not be readily understood by your readers or listeners. If a vivid quote contains slang either explain it in brackets or give a paraphrased version as well, e.g. "*He's in the cat-bird seat (in a favoured position)*" or *Saying Bush was in a favoured position, he added: "He's in the cat-bird seat."*

slugs   A slug is a word or combination of words and numerals appearing on the first line of every news agency story which uniquely identifies that story. No two stories appearing on the file in the same

24-hour news cycle should carry the same slug. News agencies often give a general indication of subject matter in the form of a generic masterslug, followed by a slug specific to that story, e.g. *OIL-LIBYA*. When a large number of stories are filed on a related issue an agency may have a triple-decker slug, e.g. *SUMMIT-ISRAEL-SHAMIR*.

sneak *sneaked* not *snuck*.

soft copy Stories, both spot and feature, that are not based on a hard news development. By giving a human perspective to political or economic developments they form an essential part of a well-rounded newspaper or news bulletin.

soft lead A soft lead seizes on a subsidiary point, usually with a strong human interest element, to entice a reader into a story, e.g. *It was not one of Kansas farmer Joe Meyer's better days. He overslept and missed breakfast, his car had a flat tyre and when he finally got to town he found that his local savings bank had gone broke.*

Soft leads are fine on features and on stories analysing the human dimension of political or economic developments and on serial stories where there has been no major recent news. But on significant news developments use a hard lead, i.e. the key facts with essential interpretation or background.

Somali Not *Somalian*.

some Write *about 500 people* rather than *some 500 people*. As an indication that a figure is an approximation, *some* is more likely to confuse translators than *about*.

song titles House styles vary but you normally put the title in quotation marks, whether or not it is italicised, and capitalise every word in it apart from conjunctions, articles, particles and short prepositions, e.g. *"I Left My Heart in San Francisco"*.

sophisticated A modish word when applied to weapons. Most weapon systems are sophisticated nowadays. If you just mean *modern*, say so.

source material Notes, tapes and other source material relating to published interviews should be saved for two years. Source material for stories that might be legally sensitive should also be saved for two years and that for other used stories for at least 48 hours.

sourcing   You should source every story clearly and explicitly for two reasons: to enable your readers or listeners to form their own judgment of its credibility and to protect your company's reputation if a story is challenged.

Any contentious statement must be rigorously sourced. On the other hand you should not blunt the impact of a story, and particularly of a lead, by excessive and intrusive sourcing if the facts are not in dispute.

However well sourced a story is, you must ensure that it is credible, impartial and legally safe.

When to source:

Ideally you should source every statement in every story unless it is an established fact or is information clearly in the public domain, like a first-hand court report or this example:

A heavy explosion shook the centre of Belfast on Thursday and a thick column of smoke rose over the area of the city's police headquarters.

An event of this kind would clearly be public knowledge. But if the explosion were in a town where there were no journalists able to write freely you would need a source, e.g.:

A heavy explosion shook the centre of Lhasa on Thursday and a thick column of smoke rose over the area of the city's police headquarters, according to reports from residents of the Tibetan capital telephoned to Beijing.

A story giving casualty figures should be sourced since such information would not be public knowledge.

However, if an event is not contentious it may be legitimate to begin a story with a paragraph that does not contain a source, as long as the sourcing is clearly given high in the story.

Location of sourcing:

Sourcing should come high in every story and in the lead if the item is contentious. If it is highly inflammatory or is an allegation seriously open to question give the source first. Write: *President Black of Ruritania accused President White of Slobbovia of genocide* not *President White of Slobbovia has committed genocide, President Black of Ruritania said.*

If the source of a story is a major figure then you should also usually put the source at the start. The same is true if the source is a weak one.

If responsibility for a statement is clear, do not repeat sourcing unnecessarily. But you must source a contentious statement or background, or at least qualify it with a word like *alleged*, each time it appears. In weaving background into a story do not attribute it to the source of the spot news.

Statements of the obvious:

There is no need to source statements of the obvious, e.g. *Destruction of half its air force is a serious blow to Ruritania, military analysts said.*

Gradation of sources:

A member of your staff or another reliable eyewitness is the best source. Next best is a named source. The weakest sources are unnamed ones. Responsibility for reporting what they say is yours alone. Unnamed sources rank as follows, in order of strength:

1. An *authoritative source* exercises real authority on the issue in question. A defence minister is an authoritative source on defence matters but not necessarily on finance.
2. An *official source* has access to information in his official capacity. But his competence as a source is limited to his field of activity.
3. *Designated sources* are, for instance, *diplomatic sources, conference sources, intelligence sources* or *sources in the mining industry.* As with an official source they must have access to reliable information on the subject in question.

Specifics of sourcing:

1. A source identified by name as well as by position carries more weight, e.g. *police spokesman John Smith* rather than a *police spokesman.* But use this technique for stories of substance and contentious statements, not for routine information of a secondary nature.
2. Cite *a source*, not *sources*, if you have only one informant.
3. Quote *a diplomat* not *diplomatic sources, an official* not *official sources.* Unless the information has been expressly given on an unattributable basis write *police said* rather than *police sources said.*
4. Be as specific as possible, e.g. *an official who was at the meeting* rather than *an official source, an army officer at the scene* rather than *military sources, German Defence Ministry officials* rather than *NATO*

sources. Do not use plain *analysts* at first reference; explain their area of expertise, e.g. *political analysts, military analysts, share analysts.*

5. Use the phrase *who declined to be named* when you have to make clear that a source insisted on anonymity. You need not use it as a tag every time you quote a diplomat or banker.

6. If your information comes from various unnamed sources you need not source each item. Give a generic sourcing, e.g. *Interviews with members of the different guerrilla groups showed a deep split on the issue. Some wanted. . . .*

7. Avoid the vague *reliable sources, well-informed sources, sources, quarters, circles* or *observers.*

Expressions of opinion and vituperative attacks:

If quoting unnamed sources on one side of a conflict about what is happening on the other side use them only for facts not opinions.

If an informant wants to make a vituperative attack on an individual, organisation or country he must speak on the record.

You should waive this rule only if the source is a senior official making a considered policy statement that is obviously newsworthy. Your story must make clear both that the informant has volunteered the information and that he is an official. If he will not speak on that basis you should consider carefully whether or not to use the story.

Such a story might begin: *Ruritania on Wednesday accused Slobbovia of practising genocide against its ethnic minorities.* The second para would then read something like this: *In a press briefing a government official, who declined to be identified, said. . . .*

Hopes and fears:

Do not use phrases that suggest you are taking sides in a dispute, e.g.: *Hopes rose that OPEC would set a lower benchmark price for oil.* You must make clear whose hopes these are.

But you can share unsourced the hopes and fears of common humanity, e.g. *Fears were mounting that 132 miners trapped. . . .*

Circumstances of statements:

Make clear how information is obtained, e.g. *said in a statement, told reporters in answer to questions* or *said in a letter to shareholders.*

Do not use passive sourcing, e.g. *it was announced, it was believed, it was understood.*

Always try to match a press report rather than simply pick it up from the newspaper. If you do quote such a report, tell the reader the result of your attempts to verify it.

Reports:

Do not use reports or unconfirmed reports as the basis for a story. You can quote an acceptable source commenting on them, e.g. *The minister said he could not confirm reports that 100 people had died.* . . .
See also **concealing sources, press reports, unnamed sources.**

South African names   Use the same style as for European names (**q.v.**).

Soviet cities   Several formerly Soviet cities have restored pre-revolutionary names changed by the Communists. They include:
Bishkek (Frunze), Gyandzha (Kirovabad), Izhevsk (Ustinov), Naberezhniye Chelny (Brezhnev), Nizhny Novgorod (Gorky), St Petersburg (Leningrad), Sergiev Posad (Zagorsk), Tver (Kalinin), Vladikavkaz (Ordzhonidize), Volgograd (Stalingrad), Yekaterinburg (Sverdlovsk).
You should use the restored name, but when helpful *(formerly Leningrad)* etc. could be added after the first reference. In historical references to World War Two, use *Siege of Leningrad* and *Battle of Stalingrad*.

soybean   Not *soyabean*.

spaces   Full stops, commas, colons and semi-colons should be followed by a single space. The same applies to close quotation marks unless followed by a punctuation mark.

Spanish names   See **Hispanic names**.

SPD   Sozialdemokratische Partei Deutschlands (German Social Democratic Party).

split infinitive   Avoid splitting infinitives if you can but do not hesitate to use a split infinitive if the alternative is an unnatural word order. *The president vowed to ruthlessly crush all armed opposition* reads better than *ruthlessly to crush* or *to crush ruthlessly.*

spokesman, spokeswoman   Not *spokesperson*. Name spokesmen or spokeswomen when they are well known in their own right, e.g. Marlin Fitzwater, or when they are providing vivid quotes or handling extemporaneously complex questions on serious issues. There is no need to name them if they are simply the mouthpieces for routine statements or for information on minor matters.

spurn   An emotive word to be avoided. Use *reject*.

square foot   To convert roughly to square metres divide by 11, precisely multiply by 0.93 (See **measures** for this and next four entries).

square metre   To convert roughly to square yards multiply by 6 and divide by 5, precisely multiply by 1.196.

square kilometre   To convert roughly to square miles multiply by 3 and divide by 8, precisely multiply by 0.386.

square mile   To convert roughly to square kilometres multiply by 8 and divide by 3, precisely multiply by 2.59.

square yard   To convert roughly to square metres multiply by 5 and divide by 6, precisely multiply by 0.836.

Sri Lanka   A Tamil rebel group, the Liberation Tigers of Tamil Eelam (LTTE), is fighting to set up an independent homeland in northern and eastern Sri Lanka for the minority Tamil community, who form 13 per cent of the island's 16 million population. The government has offered to redress Tamil grievances by devolving power to a provincial northeast council. The Tigers have rejected the offer and are waging an armed campaign for a separate state, to be called Eelam.

SST   supersonic transport.

St Petersburg   Formerly *Leningrad*, second city of Russia. In 1991 it resumed the name under which it was capital of the tsars.

stagflation   Recession, stagnation or severe slowdown in economic growth that is accompanied by steep inflation.

Stalingrad   Now *Volgograd*.

stanch   Use *staunch* for both verb and adjective. See **staunch**.

START   Strategic Arms Reduction Talks. U.S. and Soviet negotiators have been conducting these in Geneva since 1982. The treaty will cover long-range and land-based and submarine-launched missiles and long-range bombers. It sets a nominal ceiling of 1,600 launchers and 6,000 warheads, meaning a de facto cut of about one third in superpower strategic arsenals. It is the first treaty to actually reduce the number of strategic weapons.

statistical multiplexer (statmux) Unlike a time-division multiplexer (TDM), this can reassign bandwidth and so effectively carry more traffic than most TDMs.

staunch An emotive word to be used with care since it implies approval, as in *a staunch anti-Communist*.

Stealth Note capital. Current (1992) U.S. Stealth aircraft are the F-117A fighter (in fact a small bomber flown by a single pilot and designed for night attack on ground targets, not aerial warfare) and the larger B-2 "flying-wing" bomber with a crew of two or three. Both planes are subsonic. They depend for their safety on carbon-based composite building materials and an unusual shape. These either absorb radar signals or reflect them at angles that make the aircraft difficult to detect for useful periods of time.

STOL short take-off and landing.

store and forward A messaging technique in which data is received and held for subsequent retransmission, as opposed to real-time communication.

storey, story *a five-storey building* but *the story of his life*. In North American and Japan the first floor or storey is what the rest of the world would call the ground floor; likewise an American second floor is the first floor elsewhere.

storms A *storm* is more severe than a *gale*. The most severe of all storms is a *cyclone*, in which winds blow spirally inwards towards a centre of low barometric pressure. The word is used of such storms in the Indian Ocean and Australia. In the China Seas and West Pacific such a storm is called a *typhoon* and in the Caribbean and on the east coast of the United States a *hurricane*. A tornado is a violent whirling windstorm with a very narrow focus, common in the United States.

In many countries meteorological offices give tropical storms the names of men and women in alphabetical sequence. Japan numbers them sequentially, beginning afresh on January 1 each year.

To be recognised as a typhoon, a tropical storm has to have winds of 17 metres (56 feet) per second or stronger.

This is the Beaufort scale, which measures wind speed.

Force	Knots	Usual Description
0	0	Calm
1	1–3	Light air
2	4–6	Light breeze
3	7–10	Gentle breeze
4	11–16	Moderate breeze
5	17–21	Fresh breeze
6	22–27	Strong breeze or wind
7	28–33	Near-gale
8	34–40	Gale
9	41–47	Strong gale
10	48–55	Storm
11	56–63	Violent storm
12	over 63	Hurricane

Hong Kong has the following system of numbers to identify the proximity of a typhoon:

1 – A typhoon is within 400 miles of Hong Kong and may affect it.

3 – Winds gusting up to 60 knots are either imminent or already blowing. Schools close and ferry services are suspended, ships move to typhoon-proof anchorages or shelters.

8 – Gale or storm-force winds of sustained speeds of up to 63 knots, gusting to 100 knots. Government offices, businesses and public transport shut down. People in low-lying areas are evacuated. The signal means a typhoon will hit or come close to Hong Kong.

10 – Hurricane-force winds gusting in excess of 120 knots are imminent and the typhoon will hit directly.

strafe   To machinegun or rocket from the air. Do not use in referring to aerial bombing or ground-to-ground attacks.

strait-jacket   Not *straight-jacket*.

strategic   *strategy* refers to the conduct of a military campaign, *tactics* to manoeuvrings in the presence of the enemy. The distinction is worth preserving. Do not abuse *strategic* by making it mean simply important. A mountain pass, a bridge or even a building is of *strategic* importance if its possession could affect the conduct of a campaign as a whole. If it is only of local importance its value is *tactical*.

strike action   Use *strike*.

submachinegun One word. See **weapons**.

submarine In naval parlance a boat rather than a ship.

subway, subway train Use *underground railway, underground train*.

Sudan Not *the Sudan*.

sufficient Generally prefer *enough*.

sulphur Not *sulfur*.

summit Use this term only for meetings of heads of state or government. You cannot have a summit of foreign ministers or of trade union leaders. Do not use *mini-summit*. Two men can make a summit, as Bush and Gorbachev regularly showed.

Sunni Moslems are split into two main groups, Sunni and Shia.

Sunnis, the orthodox majority, are estimated at about 80 per cent of all Moslems and include the vast majority of Arabs. As well as adhering to the revelations of the Moslem holy book, the Koran, they follow the Prophet Mohammad's rule of life (the Sunna) and traditions based on his sayings.

Shias (also known as Shi'ites) give weight mostly to the Koran and the interpretations of their theologians. They hold that the headship of Islam should remain always in the Prophet's own family. Since the direct line was broken not long after the death of Mohammad, Shias believe there is a Hidden Imam who will reappear one day. In Iran, where Shias are predominant, the late Ayatollah Khomeini was considered the Imam's deputy on earth. His successor as Supreme Leader holds the same authority. The two groups draw from the same ultimate source but Shia theologians have much greater freedom of interpretation.

superlatives Avoid superlatives if they constitute value judgments. It is not your business to make them in hard news stories. Be careful with such descriptions as *first, largest, biggest, highest* and *oldest* as they can often be challenged.

Be particularly sceptical about press releases claiming records, especially auction records.

supersede Not *supercede*.

Surinam Not *Suriname*, former Dutch colony in South America.

Sverdlovsk　Now again *Yekaterinburg*, where Nicholas II, last tsar of Russia, and his family were murdered by the Bolsheviks in 1918.

swap　Not *swop*.

Szczecin　Not *Stettin*, Poland.

T

table   Do not use as a verb. It has conflicting meanings – *to put a bill forward for discussion* and *to postpone discussion of a bill*.

tables   Tables are useful means of displaying complex statistics in an easily assimilated form. For instance, a story about projected population levels in major countries could take several paragraphs to explain what could be set out simply in a table like this:

WORLD'S TWO MOST POPULOUS COUNTRIES
(IN MILLIONS)

	1985	2000	2025
China	1,059	1,285	1,492
India	769	1,042	1,445

tactical   See **strategic**.

Tangier   Not *Tangiers*, Morocco.

tanks   Use hyphens with alphanumeric designations like *M-60*, *T-62*.

target   *targeted*.

Tatar   Ethnic group. Not *Tartar*.

Tbilisi   Not *Tiflis*, Georgia.

TDM   Time-division multiplexer. See **multiplexer**.

technical terms   Be wary of using technical terms with which average readers may be unfamiliar. They are more likely to be irritated by your opacity than impressed by your knowledge. Some technical terms rapidly pass into the common language and are widely understood. These can be used freely, as long as they are used correctly in an appropriate context, literal or metaphorical, e.g. *jet lag, sound barrier, syndrome*. Others are so technical, e.g. *contra-indicate, zero-coupon bond*, or are so widely misused or misunderstood, e.g. *parameter*, that they should be briefly explained. When in doubt it is better to add a few lines of explanation, e.g. *The bends, a potentially fatal blood condition brought about when divers are brought up too quickly from great depths.* e.g. *Meltdown, overheating of radioactive fuel in a nuclear reactor to the extent that it burns through the reactor casing and escapes. . . .*

Avoid trendy use of technical terms to give your copy a spurious flavour of expertise, e.g. *black hole, modalities, throughput.*

See also **jargon**.

Tehran   Not *Teheran*, Iran.

Tel Aviv   Tel Aviv is not the capital of Israel and the status of Jerusalem is contentious. Do not use the name of either city as a synonym for Israel, as in *the Jerusalem government.*

Teletex   High-speed telex.

Teletext   A system that uses a section of a television channel to broadcast text and fairly crude graphics in page-by-page form. See also **videotex**.

television   Television is a valuable reporting aid of which journalists in other media should make full use. It is often quicker and easier to report news conferences, etc., from live television than by using even the best technology like cellular phones.

Live television can provide vivid descriptive for running stories like air crashes. A few words on rescue efforts or the colour of an aircraft fuselage add immeasurably to official figures and quotes and

can often be filed before your organisation's first correspondent arrives on the scene.

Although extended use of television coverage, and especially a television journalist's descriptive, commentary or exclusive interview, should be clearly attributed, you need not source descriptive material taken from television or quotes spoken on camera. A news conference or rescue efforts are public events.

temperatures These can be expressed, depending on your house style, in Celsius (which is the same scale as Centigrade) or in Fahrenheit. The usual convention is to use first the scale of the country involved, with conversion to your domestic scale following in brackets. Abbreviate to *C* and *F*. Freezing point in Celsius is 0 degrees, in Fahrenheit 32 degrees above zero.

Convert from Celsius to Fahrenheit for temperatures above zero by multiplying by 9, dividing by 5 and adding 32, e.g. 20 Celsius (68 Fahrenheit). For temperatures below zero Celsius multiply by 9, divide by 5 and subtract from 32, e.g. minus 15C (5F), minus 20C (minus 4F).

Convert from Fahrenheit to Celsius for temperatures above 32 by subtracting 32, multiplying by 5 and dividing by 9. For temperatures below freezing take the total number of degrees by which the temperature is below 32, multiply by 5 and divide by 9, e.g. minus 8F is 40 below freezing, 40×5/9 gives you 22, therefore minus 22C.

Temple Mount A 14-hectare (34-acre) area of the Old City of Jerusalem sacred alike to Jews and Moslems. It is the site of the biblical Jewish temple destroyed in AD 70. Jews believe the Wailing (Western) Wall below the Mount, Judaism's holiest place, is a remnant of the retaining wall of the ancient temple site. Moslems later made the Mount al-Haram al-Sharif (the Noble Sanctuary), the most important Islamic site apart from Mecca and Medina. It contains two mosques, al-Aqsa and the gold-coloured Dome of the Rock. Moslems believe the prophet Mohammad ascended into heaven from the Temple Mount.

See also **Holy Places**.

temporary respite Tautological. A respite is by definition temporary.

tenses See **indirect speech**.

terrorism On this highly emotive issue the media are always open to challenge. Do you call a gunman a terrorist or a freedom fighter?

Do you brand a guerrilla attack on a bus as terrorist but not the indiscriminate bombing of a village by government aircraft?

The most conservative and neutral policy is to abstain from all judgments and to use neutral terminology, for instance referring to terrorism in general but not, unless actually quoting someone, labelling any individual, group or action as terrorist.

Unless your house style is different prefer a neutral term like *guerrillas* to *terrorists* or, where it is possible to be more specific, *gunmen, bombers,* etc.

Tet   See **lunar new year**.

TGWU   Transport and General Workers Union (U.K.).

Thai names   The first name is used alone at second reference, e.g. *Prime Minister Anand Panyarachun said . . . Anand added. . . .*

that, which   Use *that* in defining clauses, e.g. *The horse that won the race had a white mane.* Reserve *which* for informative clauses, e.g. *The cup, which was blue, was full of water.* In other words if a clause cannot be deleted without removing information essential to the meaning of the sentence preface it with *that*. If the information in the clause is dispensable then preface it with *which*. Avoid the unnecessary use of *that* as in *He said that he was going to. . . .*

Thimphu   Not *Thimpu*, Bhutan.

Third World   Non-aligned countries of Asia, Africa and Latin America. The Second World is (or was) Soviet-led East Europe. Some talk of a Fourth World, comprising the poorest countries of the Third World.

thrash, thresh   *thrash* means to beat soundly, *thresh* to beat out corn.

threshold   Not *threshhold*.

Tibet   A vast Himalayan region of about two million people over which China says it has held sovereignty since the 13th century, a claim rejected by many Tibetans. Rebellions and protests against Chinese rule have erupted periodically since the 1950s when Communist troops took control. Martial law was imposed in the regional capital, Lhasa, in March, 1989, and lifted 13 months later.
See also **Dalai Lama**.

Tiflis   Use *Tbilisi*, Georgia.

Tigray   Not *Tigre*, Ethiopia. Adjective is *Tigrayan*.

Timbuktu   Not *Timbuktou* or *Timbuctoo*, Mali.

time   These are the conventional abbreviations of some of the world's main time zones:

> BST (British Summer Time) = GMT+1
> CET (Central European Time) = GMT+1
> EST (Eastern Standard Time) = GMT−5
> PST (Pacific Standard Time) = GMT−8

When referring to times in copy first give the local time by the 12-hour clock (but without using the words local time) and then, if necessary, follow it with a bracketed conversion to a 24-hour clock time for a specified time zone, e.g. . . .*will meet at 10 a.m. (1600 GMT).*

time element   Every story must say when events described happened. This is the time element and normally comes in the first or second paragraph.

Avoid phrases like *several months ago* or *recently* which suggest either that you do not know exactly when something happened or have been too lazy to find out. Be precise – *last August, on February 2.*

tipping   See **insider trading**.

titles   See **courtesy titles, nobility, religious titles, royalty**.

told reporters   Use this only when sources are speaking informally to a group of reporters. If they are addressing a news conference, say so.

ton, tonne   Both ton and tonne are used, normally without giving a conversion, but you must make clear what kind of ton(ne) is meant, using the terms long and short where appropriate. The three measures are:

long ton	2,240 pounds (1,016 kg)
tonne	2,204.6 pounds (1,000 kg), formerly called metric ton
short ton	2,000 pounds (907 kg), American ton

See also **measures**.

tonnage of ships   Express the size of passenger liners, cruise ships and other vessels, other than warships, tankers and dry bulk cargo ships, in gross registered tonnage (grt). This is a measurement of volume, expressed in tons, and is the first bold-type figure in Lloyd's Register of Shipping.

For tankers and dry bulk cargo vessels the measurement is in deadweight tonnes (dwt), the actual weight in metric tonnes of maximum cargo, stores, fuel and people carried, which can be at least twice the gross tonnage.

For warships the measurement is displacement tons.

You may have to distinguish between deadweight tonnes (dwt) and gross registered tons (grt), especially when reporting marine mishaps. Dwt indicates how much the ship can carry in its holds and on deck (including cargoes, bunker fuel, drinking water, food, and crew) and is used to show the size of tankers, bulk carriers and other types of vessels whose purpose is to transport goods, not passengers. Grt shows the gross volume of the ship excluding that of facilities needed for the voyage. The implications of collisions, oil spills or new ships launched are judged by dwt for tankers and bulkers, by grt for passenger liners and by displacement tons for warships. One exception is that grt is used in statistics for new ship orders because grt reflects production volume better than dwt.

A tonnage scale called compensated gross tons (cgt) is used in statistics to show a country's shipbuilding capacity. Cgt factors in manpower and added values. For instance, a VLCC is bigger and may need more steel than a smaller liquefied gas carrier, but man hours needed to complete the gas carrier, and its value in the market, may be greater than for the supertanker.

In some cases other means of measuring the ship's capacity are used. For liquefied gas carriers, cubic metres (feet) is used more often than dwt to show the capacity of the ship. For container ships teu (twenty-foot equivalent unit) and feu (forty-foot equivalent unit) are often used. Shipping officials prefer these to dwt as they show how many containers the ship can carry.

top   Use sparingly as it is often tautological, e.g. *Bush met his top aides*. . . . He would hardly consult junior aides.

torch   Do not use as a verb. Write *set on fire* or *set ablaze*.

tornado   tornadoes. See **storms**. However, the plural of the fighter-bomber in service with some West European air forces is *Tornados*.

torpedo   *torpedoes* but *torpedoing*.

Touareg   Use *Tuareg*.

trademark A trademark is a brand, symbol or word registered by a manufacturer and protected by law to prevent others from using it. Use a generic equivalent unless the trademark is important to the story.

When used, follow the owner's capitalisation, e.g. *Aspro* not *aspro* but *aspirin* not *Aspirin*.

Here is a list of common registered trademarks which are sometimes the subject of uncertainty about status, spelling or capitalisation:

adidas (note lower-case a)	sports wear
Ansafone	answering machines
Aspro	aspirin analgesic
Autocue	teleprompter
Band-Aid	sticking plaster
Biro	ball point pen
Burberry	mackintosh
Calor	bottled gas
Caterpillar	continuous-tread vehicle
Cellophane	cellulose film
Coca-Cola	cola
Courtelle	acrylic fibre
Crimplene	polyester filament yarn
Dacron	polyester fibre
Dettol	antiseptic disinfectant
Dictaphone	dictating machine
Dinky	miniature toy vehicle
Distalgesic	analgesic
Dolby	noise reduction circuitry
Dormobile	minibus
Dralon	acrylic fibre
Dunlopillo	resilient foam
Dymo	embossing tool, tape
Elastoplast	sticking plaster
Fibreglas	Owens Corning glass fibre
Fibreglass	glass fibre
flexitime	flexible work time systems
Flextime	one specific such system
Flymo	hover mowers
Formica	laminate
Hoover	vacuum cleaner

Instamatic	cartridge camera
Jacuzzi	whirlpool bath
Jiffy bag	postal bag
Kleenex	paper tissues
KiloStream	digital communications
Land Rover	all-purpose vehicle
Lego	interlocking toy bricks
Letraset	dry transfer lettering
Levi's	jeans
Linotype	hot-metal composing machine
Meccano	assembly kit toy
MegaStream	digital communications
Mini	the original BMC minicar
Nescafe	instant coffee
Orlon	acrylic fibre
Pentothal	barbiturate for anaesthesia
Perspex	acrylic sheet
Photostat	photocopier
Plasticine	modelling clay
Polaroid	filters, cameras, sunglasses
Portakabin	portable building
Primus	stove, heater
Pyrex	heat resistant glass
Range Rover	all-purpose vehicle
Scotch Tape	a transparent adhesive tape
Sellotape	a transparent adhesive tape
Spam	chopped pork and ham
Teflon	a non-stick coating on pans
Terylene	polyester fibre
Thermos	vacuum flask
Triplex	safety glass
Vaseline	petroleum jelly
Velcro	press-together fastening
Xerox	photocopier
Yellow Pages	business telephone directory

traffic   *trafficked, trafficker.*

trans-   There is no consistency of style in handling words beginning with *trans-*. But for clarity hyphenate words beginning with *trans-* if the rest of the word begins with an *s*, e.g. *trans-Siberian*. Capitalise *trans-* if the whole word refers to a geographical region, e.g. *Transcaucasus* (not *Transcaucasia*). Otherwise usage varies, e.g. *transatlantic* is generally accepted while *trans-Pacific* seems still to be the norm.

transpired It means *came to be known* not *happened*. Correct: *It transpired that at the meeting there had been a sharp disagreement over the border issue.* Wrong: *What transpired next came as a complete surprise to both sides.*

transponder The device on a satellite that receives and retransmits a signal. Transponders are usually rented from satellite operators.

transportation Use *transport* except where part of a title, e.g. *U.S. Department of Transportation.*

travel *travelled, traveller.*

trillion One thousand billion. The word should be spelled out. See also **billion**.

triplets Be careful when linking triple ideas that you have a proper complement of verbs. The following sentence is wrong: *One man was killed, hundreds of trees uprooted, and power lines blown down by the storm.* The singular verb *was* cannot govern the plural nouns *trees* and *power lines*. It should be: *One man was killed and hundreds of trees were uprooted and power lines blown down by the storm.*

troops Use for large, round numbers of soldiers not for small, specific figures. *France sent 2,000 troops to Zaire* is right; *Guerrillas killed seven government troops* is wrong.

true facts Tautological. If a fact is not true it is not a fact.

try and Use *try to.*

tsar Not *czar.*

TUC Trades Union Congress (U.K.). Note plural *Trades.*

Turkestan Not *Turkistan.*

Tuvalu Formerly Ellice Islands, West Pacific.

typhoon See **storms**.

tyre Not *tire* (of a wheel).

Tyrol Not *Tirol*, Austria.

U

UAE United Arab Emirates.

UAW United Auto Workers (U.S.).

UFO unidentified flying object.

UHF ultra high frequency.

UKAEA U.K. Atomic Energy Authority.

Ukraine Both *Ukraine* and *the Ukraine* are used. Reuter style is *Ukraine*.

Ulster See **Northern Ireland**.

umlaut House styles usually require the umlaut (two dots over an inflected vowel) in German words if it is used in the original language. If your newspaper's type face does not include the umlaut symbol, the convention is to indicate its presence by adding an *e* to the inflected vowel, e.g. *von Weizsaecker* not *von Weizsacker*, *Fuehrer* not *Fuhrer*.

U.N. United Nations.

unconventional weapons Those that deliver high explosives by unconventional means. *Non-conventional weapons* are those that carry atomic, biological or chemical warheads.

UNCTAD U.N. Conference on Trade and Development.

under way Two words. Write *began* rather than *got under way* unless referring to ships.

UNDRO U.N. Disaster Relief Office, set up in Geneva in 1971 as the focal point in the U.N. system for disaster relief. Its formal name is the Office of the United Nations Disaster Relief Coordinator. It co-ordinates aid from the world community whenever a major natural disaster occurs and the country affected requests such assistance. It also helps coordinate humanitarian relief for man-made disasters such as the crisis caused by the Iraqi invasion of Kuwait.

UNEP U.N. Environment Programme.

UNESCO U.N. Educational, Scientific and Cultural Organisation (Paris).

UNHCR U.N. High Commissioner for Refugees. If you wish to avoid using this cumbersome title at first reference use a form of words like *a U.N. agency said* or *the responsible U.N. agency said*, giving the full name lower in the story. Note that there is no U.N. High Commission for Refugees, the correct title of the institution being *the Office of the UNHCR*.

UNICEF U.N. International Children's Emergency Fund.

UNIDO U.N. Industrial Development Organisation.

uninterested, disinterested *uninterested* means the opposite of interested. If you are *disinterested* you are impartial.

unique You cannot qualify uniqueness. Never write *almost unique, more unique, rather unique*.

United Kingdom The United Kingdom comprises Great Britain and Northern Ireland. Great Britain comprises England, Wales and Scotland. Use the full or abbreviated form (*U.K.*) in media services only when it is necessary to emphasise the inclusion of Northern Ireland with England, Scotland and Wales or if you are hard-pressed for space in a headline.

United Nations Spell it out at first reference when used as a noun. As an adjective it can be abbreviated at first reference, e.g. *the U.N. General Assembly, U.N. High Commissioner for Refugees*.

United States It is normal to spell it in full when used as a noun. It may be abbreviated to *U.S.* in a headline. As an adjective it is usually abbreviated. Do not use *USA* except in quoted passages. Do not use the noun *America* as a synonym for *the United States* although you may use *American* instead of *U.S.* as an adjective.

unnamed sources Reporters should seek a named source wherever possible for any information that needs attribution. You have to accept information from two categories of unnamed sources: officials seeking to promote a particular viewpoint under the cloak of anonymity and those people whose careers, liberty or even life might be at risk if they were identified as the source of the information they give. In both cases once you have pledged not to identify a source you have an ethical obligation to protect your informant even when threatened with legal sanctions.

Treat with reserve all information given you on a non-attributable basis. Remember that if it is challenged it is your credibility that is on the line. Even if you cannot identify a source, give the reader as much guidance as you can about the possibility of bias, e.g. *A NATO official briefing German journalists on condition of anonymity said. . . . A Western official* is a weak source; *a U.S. official* is better; *a U.S. Treasury official who sat in on the negotiations* is better still.

See also **sourcing**.

unparallelled   Use *unparalleled*.

UNRWA   U.N. Relief and Works Agency for Palestinian Refugees.

uplink   The earth-to-satellite element of a satellite link.

upsurge   Use *surge*.

Uppsala   Not *Upsala*, Sweden.

urgents   A term used by news agencies to indicate a short, high-priority story less important than a flash or bulletin (**q.q.v.**).

USDA   U.S. Department of Agriculture.

USIS   U.S. Information Service.

Uzbekistan   Not *Uzbegistan*.

V

Valletta   Not *Valetta*, Malta.

Vanuatu   Formerly *New Hebrides*, Southwest Pacific.

VAT   value added tax.

VDT, VDU   Video display terminal, video display unit, usually called a CRT (cathode ray tube) in the United States.

venal, venial   A *venal* person is corruptible, a *venial* sin is pardonable.

verbs   The verb is the most important word in any sentence, giving it its essential thrust. It should, whenever possible, be active not passive (*The man shot the cat . . .* not *The cat was shot by the man*), short not long (*showed* not *demonstrated*), graphic not bureaucratic (*heading north* not *proceeding in a northerly direction*). Never use a verb plus a noun where a verb alone will suffice (*promised* not *gave an undertaking*).

veteran   Of cars, one built in 1916 or earlier. A vintage car is one built between 1917 and 1930.

VHF   very high frequency.

videotex   Not *videotext*. A system that uses a dial-up link to display text and crude graphics page by page on a screen. See also **Teletext**.

Vietnamese boat people   See **boat people**.

Vietnamese names   Use the last name alone at second reference, e.g. *Nguyen Co Thach* is *Thach* and *Bui Tin* is *Tin*. The only exception to this rule is the late *Ho Chi Minh* (a *nom de guerre*). He is *Ho* at second reference.

vintage   See **veteran**.

Vladivostok   Not *Vladivostock*.

VOA   Voice Of America.

vogue words Beloved of the lazy or semi-literate journalist, these fog the meaning of a story with neologisms and corrupt the language. The list is endless but this sentence is a fair example of vogue writing at its most pretentious: *Hopefully proactive escalation disarmamentwise will conduce within presently ongoing parameters to an exponentially expanding interface between the leading protagonists and enable them to create an interactive ambience within which they can subsume their prestigious charismas.* If you find yourself writing like this, look for another job.

voiceover A spoken report added to a television recording.

volcano *volcanoes.*

Volgograd Formerly *Tsaritsyn* and then *Stalingrad.*

VTOL vertical take-off and landing.

W

wagon Not *waggon*.

waiver, waver A *waiver* is an act of renunciation, to *waver* is to vacillate.

war *World War One, World War Two*, not *WWI, WWII*.

war reporting Many newspapers and radio and television stations have their own rules on how their staff should conduct themselves in danger areas. These are the guidelines used by Reuters in war zones where the journalist is not working as an accredited war correspondent, whether with or without a military escort from the regular army. But the general principles hold good for all war reporting and for conduct in other dangerous situations.

Your safety is paramount. You have total discretion not to go into any danger zone, even under escort. While all war reporting involves an inevitable element of risk, you must avoid obvious danger and not take unreasonable risks. You may be able to write as good a story at a safe distance as from the front line. No story, and no news picture, is worth a journalist's life.

Unless timely communication with your superiors is impossible you may move into a trouble zone only with their authorisation.

They are responsible for your safety and may order you not to run risks that you may consider acceptable. Whenever you have the opportunity to do so, you must advise your base of your movements and of any significant increase in the danger you are exposed to.

Do not move alone in a danger zone. If you travel by road do so as a passenger whenever possible, using a driver known and trusted by you and your companions who is familiar with the terrain and with potential trouble spots.

Your vehicle should be identified as a press car unless that would increase rather than decrease the danger. When possible, at least two cars should travel together in case of a breakdown.

Do not travel in military or military-style vehicles unless you are with a regular army patrol.

While correspondents, photographers and camera crews from the same organisation should work closely together in trouble zones, the differing nature of their work imposes different degrees of risk on them and they may be safer working separately. Weigh up the risks involved in each situation.

You, or someone in your party, must have a good knowledge of the local language or languages. If you do not speak the language, be sure to learn some key phrases such as foreign press, journalist, friend, British, French, etc. Learn the local meaning of flags, signs, sound signals and gestures which could be important.

Seek the advice of local authorities and local residents about possible dangers.

Never carry a weapon or travel with journalists who do. Do not carry maps with markings that could be misconstrued. Be prudent in what you photograph. As a general rule seek the agreement of troops in the area before you shoot pictures.

Carry identification, including a press card, appropriate to the area where you are. Always identify yourself clearly if challenged. Never describe yourself as anything other than a journalist. Never cross the line, or give the appearance of crossing the line, between the role of journalist as impartial observer and that of participant in a conflict. If working on both sides of a front line never give information to one side about military operations on the other side.

If caught in a situation where troops are hostile and threatening towards you, cocking their weapons and so on, try to stay relaxed. Act friendly and smile. Aggressive or nervous behaviour on your part is likely to be counter-productive. Carry cigarettes or other small luxuries to use as an icebreaker.

Always wear civilian clothes unless accredited as a war correspondent and required to wear special dress. Use your judgment as to whether to dress to blend with the crowd or to be distinctively visible. In either case avoid wearing military or para-military clothing.

You may wear protective clothing such as a flak jacket or body armour as long as this does not increase the risks or encourage you to act recklessly. You should also carry a gas mask and appropriate protective clothing if entering an area where there is a possibility that biological or chemical weapons may be used.

It is worth carrying the internationally recognised bracelet available with the caduceus symbol on one side and with space on the other on which to list your blood group and any allergies.

The party with which you are travelling should have a basic first-aid kit and a supply of sterile syringes. Get some basic first-aid training before going into a danger zone or at the first subsequent opportunity.

warplane One word, by analogy with *warship*. Better to be specific and use *fighters, bombers, etc.*

warn A transitive verb. Write *Bush warned Congress that war was inevitable* or *Bush gave a warning that war was inevitable* but not *Bush warned that war was inevitable.*

Warsaw Pact An East European Communist military alliance, equivalent to NATO (**q.v.**) in the West, set up by the 1955 Warsaw Treaty and disbanded in 1991.

weapons A weapon's calibre is the internal diameter of its barrel. Express it in millimetres or decimal fractions of an inch, e.g. *a 155mm gun, a 105mm howitzer, an eight-inch gun, a .22-calibre pistol, a Colt .45.* Most shotguns are measured by their gauge; the smaller the gauge the larger and more lethal the pellets fired.

A handgun is a weapon that can be held and fired in one hand, e.g. a pistol. Rifles and shotguns are not handguns.

A pistol, e.g. *a .38-calibre Luger,* is a generic term for a small handgun. There are two kinds of pistols – a revolver, which has a rotating magazine, and an automatic, which reloads itself automatically after every shot, usually from a magazine in the butt.

A fully automatic weapon reloads itself and keeps firing as long as the trigger is being pressed. A semi-automatic reloads itself but the trigger has to be pressed separately for each shot.

A mortar is the tube from which a mortar bomb (not shell) is fired. It is not the projectile itself.

A howitzer is an artillery piece with a relatively short barrel designed to fire at a high angle over hills.

A machinegun, e.g. *a .50-calibre Dushka*, is a fully automatic weapon, normally mounted on a support. A submachinegun is also normally fully automatic, but may be used in semi-automatic mode when you have to press the trigger once for each shot.

A carbine is a short-barrelled rifle.

In describing the scene of a gun fight distinguish between bullets (the projectiles fired) and the spent cartridge cases (which contained the propellant charge). The cartridge comprises a metal cartridge case, a priming charge, the propellant and the bullet.

Hyphenate alphanumeric designations of weapons like the *AK-47*, *M-16*. Capitalise weapons systems like *ICBM, SAM*.

weather Write *good/poor/stormy weather* not *good/poor/stormy weather conditions*.

West Capitalise it when used in a political sense.

WEU Western European Union, the only purely European defence organisation, founded in 1954. Its members are Belgium, Britain, France, Germany, Italy, Luxembourg, the Netherlands, Portugal and Spain. All are members both of NATO and the European Community (**q.q.v.**). For decades little more than a talking shop, the WEU has recently become the focus of efforts to create a genuine European voice in defence and security policy, as the EC moves towards greater economic and political integration and the United States prepares to withdraw many of the troops it based in Western Europe during the Cold War. The WEU as of early 1992 had no military structure and no forces assigned to it. Its headquarters are in London but are likely to move to Brussels, the home of both NATO and the EC.

WFP World Food Programme (Rome). A branch of the U.N. Food and Agriculture Organisation, it is the U.N.'s biggest food aid agency.

whiskey, whisky *whiskey* is Irish and U.S., *whisky* is Scotch.

whiz-kid Note hyphen, one *z*.

which, that See **that, which**.

which, who   Use *which* rather than the personal pronoun *who* when writing about countries, governments, organisations and companies, e.g. *The NATO allies, which decided.* . . .

whom, whom   See **pronouns**.

WHO   World Health Organisation (Geneva).

widow   Either of these is all right – *the widow of President John Smith* or *the wife of the late President John Smith. The widow of the late President John Smith* is tautological. Use *the late* only of those recently dead, not for instance of someone like John Kennedy who has been almost 30 years in the grave.

with   Avoid this word as a connector in clumsy lead constructions like *Ruritania voted on Saturday for provincial assemblies with the Peasants Party fighting a rearguard action.* . . .

withhold   Not *withold*.

woes   Acceptable in a headline for the sake of brevity but avoid such journalese as *economic woes* in text.

World Bank   The alternative form by which the International Bank for Reconstruction and Development in Washington is usually known.

World Court   See **International Court of Justice**.

World War One/Two   Also *First/Second World War.* Not *WWI/ WWII*.

worldwide   No hyphen.

worship   *worshipper, worshipped.*

wounds   See **injuries**.

wrack, rack   Use *wrack* only for seaweed and in the phrase *wrack and ruin*. Otherwise use *rack*.

wrap   In text-handling systems this carries whole words forward to the next line, ensuring that words are not broken at the end of a line.

wrapup   A journalistic term for a comprehensive lead (**q.v.**) to a story.

XYZ

yard To convert roughly to metres multiply by 9 and divide by 10, precisely multiply by 0.914.

yardsticks The man in the street has difficulty in visualising scale. Be imaginative in helping him, e.g. *Kazakhstan, a republic five times as large as France . . . 10,000 of them would fit on a pinhead . . . The cars on Ruritania's roads, if parked nose to tail, would girdle the earth three times. . . .*

year ends Financial, fiscal (tax), company and crop years rarely coincide with calendar years so it is vital in business stories to explain clearly which year is referred to, e.g.:
The budget deficit for the financial year ended March 1990 was . . . or *Cocoa production rose 14 per cent to 700,000 tonnes in the crop year ended September 1990.*

Take care with crop year dates as the old crop can be harvested and the new crop planted in the same year. To refer to the 1990 crop can be dangerously ambiguous.

Commodity producers sometimes also have marketing years for their produce which differ from the crop year. In these cases be careful to spell out which year you are referring to and when each starts and ends.

Organisations such as the U.S. Department of Agriculture and the International Coffee Organisation may also produce statistics, for example on Brazilian coffee production, that are based on different years.

Yom Kippur The Day of Atonement, the holiest day in the Jewish calendar. Egypt launched the 1973 war on Yom Kippur, inflicting initial heavy losses on Israel in a surprise attack.

zloty Polish currency, Plural *zlotys*.

Zuider Zee Not *Zuyder Zee*, Netherlands.

Zulu A term used by Western military forces to mean GMT (**q.v.**).

APPENDIX I – CONVERSIONS

These are some of the most common approximate equivalents between metric and British and American measures:

Length

1 inch	= 2½ centimetres
1 foot	= 30 centimetres = ⅓ metre
3¼ feet	= 1 metre
39 inches	= 1 metre
11 yards	= 10 metres
⅝ mile	= 1 kilometre
5 miles	= 8 kilometres
8 miles	= 7 nautical miles

Area

1 square inch	= 6½ square centimetres
10¾ square feet	= 1 square metre
6 square yards	= 5 square metres
2½ acres	= 1 hectare
250 acres	= 1 square kilometre
3 square miles	= 8 square kilometres

Volume

1 teaspoonful	= 5 millilitres
1 U.K. fluid ounce	= 28 millilitres
26 U.K. fluid ounces	= 25 U.S. liquid ounces
1¾ U.K. pints	= 1 litre
7 U.K. pints	= 4 litres
5 U.K. pints	= 6 U.S. liquid pints
1 U.K. gallon	= 4½ litres
5 U.K. gallons	= 6 U.S. gallons
1 U.S. gallon	= 3¾ litres
3 cubic feet	= 85 litres or cubic decimetres
35 cubic feet	= 1 cubic metre
4 cubic yards	= 3 cubic metres

27½ U.K. bushels	= 1 cubic metre
28⅓ U.S. bushels	= 1 cubic metre
11 U.K. bushels	= 4 hectolitres
14 U.S. bushels	= 5 hectolitres
1 barrel (petroleum)	= 42 U.S. gallons or 35 U.K. gallons
1 barrel per day	= 50 tonnes per year

Yield

| 1 U.K. ton per acre | = 2½ tonnes per hectare |
| 9 pounds per acre | = 10 kilograms per hectare |

Weight

1 grain	= 65 milligrams
15½ grains	= 1 gram
1 ounce	= 28 grams
1 ounce troy	= 31 grams
1 pound	= 454 grams
35 ounces	= 1 kilogram
2¼ pounds	= 1 kilogram
2,205 pounds	= 1 tonne
11 U.S. tons	= 10 tonnes
100 U.K. (long) tons	= 112 U.S. (short) tons

Speed

2 miles per hour	= 3 feet per second
9 miles per hour	= 4 metres per second
11 km per hour	= 10 feet per second
30 miles per hour	= 48 kilometres per hour
50 miles per hour	= 80 kilometres per hour

Fuel consumption

5 U.K. gallons per mile	= 14 litres per kilometre
20 miles per U.K. g.	= 7 kilometres per litre
20 miles per U.K. g.	= 14 litres per 100 km
5 miles per U.S. g.	= 6 miles per U.K. gallon

Density

4 ounces per U.K. g.	= 25 grams per litre
2 ounces per U.S. g.	= 15 grams per litre
1 pound per cubic foot	= 16 kg per cubic metre

Power

4 U.K. horsepower	= 3 kilowatts
72 U.K. horsepower	= 73 metric horsepower

APPENDIX II – TECHNICAL GLOSSARY

Computer and data transmission terms commonly used by journalists are defined in the main body of the text. This appendix contains more specialised computer terminology.

acoustic coupler A device that clamps over a telephone handset to enable data to be sent by dial-up, largely superseded by the modem (**q.v.**).

A/D converter A device to convert analogue (**q.v.**) transmission to digital (**q.v.**) or vice versa.

ADP Automatic data processing.

analogue (analog) Direct representation of a phenomenon in another form, e.g. voice as a series of electrical audio signals, in contrast to digital systems, in which phenomena are represented by binary digits (bits). For news pictures, analogue transmission is a method of transmitting variations in grey-scale by varying the amplitude of a constant tone or the frequency of a tone.

ARQ protocol Automatic repeat request. This data transmission protocol guarantees error-free delivery, whatever the quality of the transmission path, by having the receiving side request retransmission of data that arrives corrupted.

buffer Temporary storage area for data, often used while it is being passed from one device to another.

bus See **minicomputer**.

CD-ROM Compact disk, read-only memory.

Coast Earth Station An Inmarsat (**q.v.**) ground station which relays satellite traffic to its destination.

CPU A computer's central processing unit, where programs are executed.

data compression   A technique that reduces the number of information bits that need to be sent. It is especially useful for transmission of pictures or large quantities of on-line data.

digital darkroom   Generic term in the United States for an electronic picture editing system.

digitise   To express as a combination of bits (**q.v.**). Adjective digital.

DOS   Disk operating system. See **operating system**.

DP   Data processing.

DRAM   Dynamic random access memory.

DTE   Data terminal equipment, any equipment at which a communication path begins or ends, e.g. keyboard and screen.

end of message   A string of characters that signal to a communications system that a message is complete. To these systems each page of a story is a separate message and needs a start-of-message and end-of-message signal. These are provided automatically by the computers linked with video-editing terminals (VDUs). If there is no VDU the signals must be typed in. The start-of-message signal is ZCZC and the EOM signal NNNN.

eprom   Erasable programmable read-only memory, a chip that can be reprogrammed only by a special device, not by the computer where it normally resides.

Ethernet   A type of local area network (see **LAN**), endorsed by European and U.S. standards bodies and some leading manufacturers.

Fifth Generation   A concept introduced in Japan to describe computer architecture using parallel processing (**q.v.**) instead of the sequential systems used hitherto. First-generation computers were very large machines using valves. The invention of the transistor in 1947 led to the second generation, and integrated circuits brought about the third in the early 1960s. The fourth generation came with large-scale integration (LSI) of at least 100 logic circuits on a single chip.

file server   A device that services all the workstations and terminals attached to a network (see **LAN**), typically consisting of a

Winchester disk, a processor and file management software. By extension, but less precisely, any computer supporting a network.
See also **server**.

firmware Computer components that are neither hardware nor software, e.g. a unit that stores information used in programming.

gateway A facility that allows the user of one computer system to communicate through it to another system.

gigabyte Measure of computer memory, roughly one billion bytes.
See **byte** and **units of measurement**.

half-duplex See **duplex**.

host The central device used in any particular computer operation.

IC card Integrated circuit card, also known as a smart card, a batch of memory chips, with no moving parts, packed in a slab the size of a credit card. IC cards offer quicker access and are lighter, smaller, more efficient and more reliable than floppy disks, which can die suddenly if scratched.

icon In news graphics a small symbol, as used on maps.

LSI Large-scale integration, i.e. the crowding of large numbers of instructions (at least 100 logic circuits) on very small chips.

mainframe An imprecise term for a larger computer at the centre of a system, which may include a number of minicomputers and other devices.

megabyte Measure of computer memory, about a million bytes.
See **byte** and **units of measurement**.

microcomputer Often synonymous with personal computer. The term originated when all the device's memory could be held on a single chip, a microprocessor.

microprocessor See **microcomputer**.

minicomputer An imprecise term for a small to medium-sized computer, usually part of a bigger system. Originally it differed from a mainframe in that all data moved in and out of a mini along a single path, known as a bus, but many mainframes also use buses now.

mips Million instructions per second, a measure of computer performance, unreliable for comparisons except between similar machines.

MS-DOS See **operating systems**.

OCR Optical character recognition, a technique for reading text into a computer from the shape of characters, as opposed to ASCII (**q.v.**).

operating system This controls the overall running of a computer. Examples are DOS, MS-DOS, UNIX.

optical disk A data storage device read by a laser beam detecting microscopic differences on its surface, more compact and reliable than floppy disks, or magnetic tapes, but more costly to write data to.

optical fibre Microscopic glass fibre through which light is transmitted to carry signals; the technique is faster and more compact than copper wire, but more costly.

OSI Open Systems Interconnection, a seven-level standard drawn up by the ISO (**q.v.**) to enable computers and other devices to talk to one another.

parallel port A digital interface, typically the point at which a circuit enters or leaves a computer, in which a separate wire is dedicated to each signal.

parallel processing Simultaneous handling by a number of devices of different elements of a computer process, e.g. a complex database search, making it much faster.

parallel transmission Method by which the bits that make up a character pass simultaneously along separate paths, as opposed to serial transmission.

parity check Part of an error control procedure in which a given number of bits is checked. Parity bits are appended to data to create an even, or sometimes an odd, parity.

peripherals All kinds of devices that can be attached to a data terminal to provide additional ways of inputting, storing or outputting data, e.g. printers, disk drives.

port The input to or output from a computer system. In different aspects ports can be described as physical or logical.

programming languages Used to write software. Among the better known are APL, Basic, Cobol, Fortran.

protocol A set of rules, implemented by devices at each end of a transmission path, defining how traffic should be passed over it.

proximity search In a database this is used to look for two or more terms that appear close to one another in text.

RAM Random access memory.

ROM Read-only memory.

RS232 Also known as V.24, the standard interface for connecting a terminal to a modem, agreed by the CCITT (**q.v.**).

selector A device, often at a client site, that reads encoded data, e.g. address codes or interest codes, to determine which services are available to a particular circuit or terminal. More advanced selectors can be reprogrammed remotely.

semiconductor A material whose electrical conductivity is between that of a metal and an insulator, e.g. silicon.

serial transmission Method by which the bits that make up a character pass one after another along the same path, as opposed to parallel transmission.

server A computer that supports a group of workstations; an editing system may have several servers.

SES Ship earth station, an Inmarsat (**q.v.**) term for a remote terminal, even if land-based, communicating with a coastal earth station.

silicon chips The basis of most logic and memory circuits in computers. Silicon is used because of its properties as a semiconductor (**q.v.**) and because it is abundant and therefore cheap.

smart card Also IC (integrated circuit) card, a batch of memory chips, with no moving parts, packed in a slab the size of a credit card. Smart cards offer quicker access and are lighter, smaller, more efficient and more reliable than floppies, which can die suddenly if scratched.

soft key A keystroke that can be programmed to perform different functions, depending what mode a computer is currently operating in.

software A logical system programmed into a computer for it to perform designated tasks.

start of message A string of characters that signal to a communications system that a new message is beginning. To these systems each page of a story is a separate message and needs a start-of-message and end-of-message signal. These are provided automatically by the computers linked with video-editing terminals (VDUs). If there is no VDU the signals must be typed in. The SOM signal is ZCZC and the end-of-message signal NNNN.

units of measurement Bits and bytes are inadequate terms for measuring systems' capacity, so compound terms are used. In computing, numbers greater than 1,000 are calculated in powers of two (e.g. 2 to the power of 10) rather than multiples of 10: the prefixes are: kilo- (1,024), mega- (1,048,576), giga- (1,073,741,824) and tera- (1,099,511,627,776). For fractions smaller than a thousandth the prefixes are: milli- (thousandth), micro- (millionth), nano- (billionth), pico- (trillionth), and femto- (thousand-trillionth).

UNIX A multi-user computer operating system.

V.24 See **RS232**.

VLSI Very large-scale integration. See **LSI**.

WAN Wide area network. This is like a LAN (**q.v.**) but is spread over a much wider area, often internationally.

Winchester disk A type of hard disk, usually not interchangeable.

window A screen facility that lets the user interrupt one function in order to perform another; it appears as a rectangular portion of the screen.

X.25 The most widely accepted CCITT packet-switching standard.

X.400 An international standard protocol for electronic mail.

APPENDIX III – BUSINESS ABBREVIATIONS

General

adj	adjusted
AFL-CIO	American Federation of Labour – Congress of Industrial Organisations
ANC	African National Congress
ASEAN	Association of Southeast Asian Nations
Benelux	Belgium, Netherlands and Luxembourg
BIS	Bank for International Settlements
bln	billion
BLS	Bureau of Labour Statistics (Washington)
B/S	building society (U.K)
CBI	Confederation of British Industry (U.K.)
CEA	(Presidential) Council of Economic Advisers (U.S.)
CGBR	central government borrowing requirement
CITIC	China International Trust and Investment Corp
CSO	Central Statistics Office (U.K.)
EPC	Economic Policy Committee of the OECD
EC	European Community
ECLA	Economic Commission for Latin America/ Caribbean
EFTA	European Free Trade Association
EIB	European Investment Bank
EX-IM Bank	Export-Import Bank (U.S.)
FAA	Federal Aviation Administration (U.S.)
GAB	General Arrangements to Borrow
GAO	General Accounting Office (U.S.)
GATT	General Agreement on Tariffs and Trade (U.N.)
HK	Hong Kong

IADB	Inter-American Development Bank
IATA	International Air Transport Association (Geneva)
IBRD	International Bank for Reconstruction and Development (World Bank)
IDA	International Development Association
IMF	International Monetary Fund
IMM	International Monetary Market (Chicago)
Insee	Institute of Economic Statistics (Paris)
intl	international
IRA	Irish Republican Army
IStat	Italian National Statistics Institute
JEC	Joint Economic Committee (U.S. House-Senate)
kg	kilogram(s)
km	kilometre(s)
kph/mph	kilometres/miles per hour
LDC	less (or least) developed country
MITI	Ministry of International Trade and Industry (Japan)
mln	million
MLR	minimum lending rate
mo	month with a figure – eg 2-mo bills (with hyphen)
NASA	National Aeronautics and Space Administration (U.S.)
NATO	North Atlantic Treaty Organisation
NBER	National Bureau of Economic Research (U.S.)
NEDC	National Economic Development Council (U.K.)
NIESR	National Institute for Economic and Social Research (U.K.)
OBU	offshore banking unit
OECD	Organisation for Economic Cooperation and Development
IC	Organisation of the Islamic Conference
OMB	Office of Management and Budget (U.S.)
qtr/qtly	quarter/quarterly
s/adj	seasonally adjusted
SEK	Swedish Export Credit
trln	trillion

UA	unit of account
UAE	United Arab Emirates
U.N.	United Nations
UNCTAD	U.N. Conference on Trade and Development
UNESCO	U.N. Educational, Scientific and Cultural Organisation
U.K.	United Kingdom
U.S.	United States
vs	versus
wk	week
yr or yr/yr	year or year-on-year
91/92	1991/92 etc

Money/futures

Bibor	Bahrain/Bangkok interbank offered rate
BOE	Bank of England
BOJ	Bank of Japan
bop	balance of payments
c/a	current account
CAF	currency adjustment factor
CBOE	Chicago Board Options Exchange
CBOT	Chicago Board of Trade
CME	Chicago Mercantile Exchange
cpi	consumer price index
FASB	Financial Accounting Standards Board (U.S.)

Currencies

Aus dlr	Australian dollar
Can dlr	Canadian dollar
cfa	Central African Franc
dlr	U.S. dollar
Ecu	European currency unit
mark	German mark
sdr	Special Drawing Right
stg	sterling
forex	foreign exchange
G7/G10/G24	Group of Seven/10/24
EMS	European Monetary System
EMU	European Monetary Union
ERM	exchange rate mechanism of the EMS
EOE	European Options Exchange (Amsterdam)

Fed	Federal Reserve System/Board (U.S.)
Fibor	Frankfurt interbank offered rate
FOMC	Federal (Reserve) Open Market Committee (U.S.)
gdp/gnp	gross domestic/national product
Hibor	Hong Kong interbank offered rate
Libor	London interbank offered rate (on eurodollars)
Luxibor	Luxembourg interbank offered rate
MOF	Ministry of Finance (Japan)
MAS	Monetary Authority of Singapore
Pibor	Paris interbank offered rate
ppi	producer price index
psbr/psdr	public sector borrowing/debt requirement
repos	repurchase agreements
rpi	retail price index
SAMA	Saudi Arabian Monetary Agency
SFE	Sydney Futures Exchange
Sibor	Singapore interbank offered rate
SIMEX	Singapore International Monetary Exchange
SRD	Statutory Reserve Deposits (Australia)
VAT	value added tax
wpi	wholesale price index
WP3	Working Party 3 of the OECD

Capital markets

AFBD	Association of Futures Brokers and Dealers (U.K.)
AIBD	Association of International Bond Dealers
c/d	certificate of deposit
cnv	convertible, as in bonds
cnv note	convertible note
cp	commercial paper
ECSC	European Coal and Steel Community
ECGD	Export Credit Guarantee Department (U.K.)
EDC	Export Development Corp (Canada)
Eurofima	European Company for the Financing of Railroad Rolling Stock
FBDB	Federal Business Development Bank (Canada)
FDIC	Federal Deposit Insurance Corporation (U.S.)

FEK	Finnish Export Credit
FHA	Federal Housing Administration (U.S.)
FHLBB	Federal Home Loan Bank Board (U.S.)
FHLMC	Federal Home Loan Mortgage Corporation (Freddie Mac – U.S.)
FIMBRA	Financial Intermediaries, Managers and Brokers Regulatory Association (U.K.)
FNMA	Federal National Mortgage Association (Fannie Mae – U.S.)
frcd	floating rate certificate of deposit
frn	floating rate note
GMAC	General Motors Acceptance Corp
GNMA	Government National Mortgage Association (Ginnie Mae – U.S.)
IBA	Investment Bankers Association (U.S.)
IFC	International Finance Corporation (Washington)
IMC	International Monetary Conference of the American Bankers' Association
IMRO	Investment Managers Regulatory Organisation (U.K.)
IPMA	International Primary Market Association
Lautro	Life Assurance and Unit Trust Regulatory Organisation (U.K.)
MTN	medium-term note/multilateral trade negotiations
nif	note issuance facility
OPIC	Overseas Private Investment Corporation (U.S.)
OTS	Office of Thrift Supervision (U.S.)
Sallie Mae	Student Loan Marketing Association (U.S.)
SIB	Securities and Investments Board (U.K.)
s/l	savings and loan
SRO	self-regulatory organisation (U.K.)
stepped coupon	stepped-up or stepped-down coupon bond
T-bills	Treasury bills
TSA	The Securities Association (U.K.)
vrn	variable rate note
wts	warrants

Equities

AB	Aktiebolag (Swedish stock company)
ADB	Asian Development Bank (Manila) and African Development Bank (Abidjan)
ADR	American Depositary Receipt
AG	Aktiengesellschaft (West German, Swiss or Austrian stock company limited by shares)
AMEX	American Stock Exchange (New York)
A/S	Aktieselskabet (Danish stock company)
attrib	attributable
avg	average
BDI	Bundesverband der Deutschen Industrie (West German Industry Association)
Bros	Brothers
BV	Besloten Vennootscap (Dutch private limited company)
Co	Company
COB	Commission des Opérations de Bourse (French Stock Exchange Commission)
Cofindustria	Confederazione Generale dell'Industria Italiana (Italian Industry Association)
COMEX	Commodity Exchange Inc (New York)
COPA	Comité des Organisations Professionnelles Agricoles de la CEE (EC farmers' lobby group)
Corp	Corporation
div	dividend
eGmbH	eingetragene Genossenschaft mit beschraenkter Haftpflicht (German registered limited liability cooperative) plus eGmuh for unlimited liability
GmbH	Gesellschaft mit beschraenkter Haftung (German limited liability company)
Inc	Incorporated
IRI	Istituto per la Ricostruzione Industriale (Italian State Holding Company)
KG	Kommanditgesellschaft (German limited partnership)
KGaA	Kommanditgesellschaft auf Aktien (German company limited by shares and with one or more general partners)

KK	Kabushiki-Kaisha (Japanese stock company)
lbo	leveraged buyout
NASDAQ	National Association of Securities Dealers Automated Quotation System (U.S.)
NL	No Liability (Australia)
NYMEX	New York Mercantile Exchange
NV	Naamloze Vennootscap (Dutch limited company with shares)
NYSE	New York Stock Exchange
oper/shr	operating profit per share
OTC	over the counter
Oy	Osakeyhtio (Finnish stock company)
Plc	Public limited company (U.K.)
PME	Petites et Moyennes Entreprises (French small/medium business association)
prelim	preliminary
prov	provisional
PT	Perusahaan Terbatas (Indonesian public limited company)
Pte	Private (Singapore company)
Pty	Proprietary (Australian company)
PSE	Pacific Stock Exchange
SA	Société Anonyme (French Corporation) and Sociedad Anonima (Spanish Corporation)
SARL	Société Anonyme à Responsabilité Limitée
S&L or S and L	savings and loan company (U.S.)
Sdn Bhd	Sendirian Berhad (Malaysian public limited company)
SEC	Securities and Exchange Commission (U.S.)
shr	earnings per share
SIA	Securities Industry Association (U.S.)
SpA	Società per Azioni (Italian limited company)
SPRI	Société de Personnes à Responsabilité Limitée (Belgian or French corporation)

Commodities

AISI	American Iron and Steel Institute (New York)
AMM	Associate Mercantile Market (Chicago)
ANRPC	Association of Natural Rubber Producing Countries

ASA	American Soyabean Association
ATPC	Association of Tin Producing Countries
BSC	British Steel Corporation
c&f	cost and freight paid to port of destination
CAP	Common Agricultural Policy (of the EC)
CCC	Commodity Credit Corporation (U.S.)
CFTC	Commodity Futures Trading Commission (U.S.)
cif	cost, insurance and freight
CIPEC	Inter-Governmental Council of Copper Exporting Countries (abbreviation of name in Spanish)
dwt	deadweight tonnes
FAO	Food and Agriculture Organisation (U.N.)
FAQ	fair average quality
FAS	free alongside ship
FDA	Food and Drug Administration (U.S.)
fio	free in and out
fios	free in and out stowed
fob	free on board
GAFTA	Grain and Feed Trade Association (U.K.)
grt	gross registered tons
HGCA	Home-Grown Cereals Authority (U.K.)
IAA	Instituto do Azucar e do Alcool (Brazilian Sugar and Alcohol Institute)
ICC	Interstate Commerce Commission (U.S.)
ICCH	International Commodities Clearing House
ICCO	International Cocoa Organisation
ICO	International Coffee Organisation
IISI	International Iron and Steel Institute
ILZSG	International Lead and Zinc Study Group
INRO	International Natural Rubber Organisation
IRSG	International Rubber Study Group
ISO	International Sugar Organisation
ITC	International Trade Commission (U.S.) and International Tin Council
IWA	International Wheat Agreement
IWC	International Wheat Council
IWCC	International Wrought Copper Council
IWS	International Wool Secretariat
IWTO	International Wool Textile Organisation

JETRO	Japan External Trade Organisation
LME	London Metal Exchange
MFA	Multi-Fibres Arrangement
MFN	most favoured nation
MTN	multilateral trade negotiations
OO	ore/oil carrier
PL480	Public Law 480, on subsidised sales of produce abroad (U.S.)
Shex	Sundays and holidays exempted (shiploading)
Shinc	Sundays and holidays included
USDA	U.S. Department of Agriculture
WWD	weather working days

Energy

API	American Petroleum Institute
bpd	barrels per day
EIA	Energy Information Administration (U.S.)
Euratom	European Atomic Energy Community
FERC	Federal Energy Regulatory Commission (U.S.)
IAEA	International Atomic Energy Agency (Vienna)
IEA	International Energy Agency (Paris)
IPE	International Petroleum Exchange
OAPEC	Organisation of Arab Petroleum Exporting Countries
OPEC	Organisation of Petroleum Exporting Countries
PDVSA	Venezuela state oil concern (energy service only)
ULCC	ultra large crude carrier
VLCC	very large crude carrier